Carpooling with Death

How living with death will make you STRONGER, WISER and FEARLESS

Margaret Meloni

www.margaretmeloni.com/carpoolingwithdeath/

ISBN hardcover: 978-1-7329075-0-8
ISBN paperback: 978-1-7329075-1-5
ISBN ebook: 978-1-7329075-2-2

"Combining practical advice and spiritual insight, humor and heartbreak, Carpooling with Death is a much needed companion on this crazy ride of living and dying. Margaret Meloni has written a moving personal account of her journey with love and loss."

- Michaela Haas, PhD, author of *Bouncing Forward* and *Dakini Power*

"Carpooling with death feels like reading a personal diary. And so it is. Author Margaret Meloni allows us to accompany her as she encounters death and impermanence throughout her life and ultimately finds that equanimity, compassion and lovingkindness help her recreate her own life."

- Sharon Salzberg, author of *Lovingkindness and real Happiness*

Dedication

Oh, the irony. The ones who inspired me, the ones who are the reason that this book exists, are not here to read it. Of course, if they were here, there would be no book. As I wrote every word, I carried them in my heart. They are the ones who spurred me on. To Mom, Dad, and Ed. Thank you, for all of your love and support. Thank you, for helping me to make friends with death.

Acknowledgments

I have come to a place where I am comfortable with death, but I have not come to a place where I have overcome the fear of forgetting to thank everyone who has helped me on this journey. And everyone who continues to help me as the journey continues. I appreciate you all. Those who knew I was writing and encouraged me to stick with it. Those who did not know, but sat with me in meditation, or shared life's adventures with me. If you are part of my life, then in some way, you helped me to create Carpooling with Death. And if you are arriving now, thank you for trusting me to introduce you to my friend, Grim.

"'All conditioned things are impermanent' — when one sees this with wisdom, one turns away from suffering." Dhp 277

Meeting Death at a Cocktail Party
(A Haiku)

So what do you do?

Harvesting souls is your gig.

Are you working now?

Table of Contents

Abbreviations

These are the abbreviations used for the Pāli Buddhist Texts which may be quoted throughout this book.

AN	Aṅguttara Nikāya
Dhp	Dhammapada
DN	Dīgha Nikāya
MN	Majjhima Nikāya
SN	Saṃyutta Nikāya
Sn	Sutta Nipāta
Thag	Theragāthā
Ud	Udāna

Introduction

There came a point in my life when I began to realize that the people I loved were going to die. My mother-in-law, Lee, was in her nineties, my parents were approaching their eighties, and my husband, Ed, had already outlived his father. I had already said goodbye to others. How could I handle losing the people I loved the most? I knew that death would come, but I was fearful that I would be unprepared. I used to tell myself that I was not afraid of *my* death; I did not want to be left behind by the ones I loved. And, yes, part of me realized just how unrealistic I was being.

At the same time, I noticed how unrealistic many of us are about death. At ninety-five, even though she was the last one left in her family, my mother-in-law had never seriously considered her death. Her passing at ninety-eight and a half was my final wake-up call. It was time to become "death ready."

The good news was that, a few years before Lee died, Ed and I had become Buddhists. We began to embrace the concept of impermanence. We learned about the cause of suffering. One of our early teachers encouraged us to consider death, to develop the understanding that each day could be our last. And then, just two years after we buried Lee, my father was diagnosed with terminal lung cancer. Initially, the oncologist gave him no more than six weeks to live. I had the opportunity to examine my attachment to wanting things to stay the same, and my aversion to dealing with death.

Around the same time, Ed began to have cancer scares. The first few were just that, scares, but I recognized that the real deal was coming. As we moved closer to Ed's death, I knew it was going to be the most challenging experience of my life. I also consoled myself with the fact that, at least for some amount of time, I would have my mother to help me. At this point, she had been a widow for about two years. She had shared some of her experiences with me. She was spunky and energetic. I envisioned spending more time visiting her after Ed's death and, if she felt up to it, taking trips together. But that was not to be. Mom died of a heart attack five days before Ed died.

Part of me was tempted to think that death had been stalking me, but being a Buddhist helped me to accept that the Grim Reaper was just doing his job. I began to accept him as part of my network. Digging into my Buddhist practice was a critical part of my recovery. It is not that I did not experience grief; I simply understood the root of my suffering and that it would not last forever. Sitting in meditation and contemplating death and grief made me stronger, and wiser.

Carpooling with Death covers my journey to accept death as a part of life, the guidance I found through my Buddhist practice and the clarity I gained in understanding where to find support and how to recreate my new life. And if I did it, then so can you. In each section of this book, I share my experiences, to give you insight into how to incorporate death into your life and how to rely on the foundations of Buddhism to see you through it all.

The journey begins in Part I, with the final moments of Dad, Mom and Ed, each moment beautiful in its own way, proof that death does not have to be frightening.

Next, in Part II, I ask you to take a step back with me and look at what it is like to live with the certainty that death is approaching. Together, we can grapple with your fear of death. You will see that fear is about uncertainty. Death is a certainty, which means there is no need for concern. Now you are free to make the most of the time that remains and to help your loved one have a good death.

Most of us do not become "death ready" at the snap of a finger. It helps to have faith. Maybe you do not associate the word faith with Buddhism, but relying on the path mapped out for us by the Buddha gave me the strength to keep going. Part III is an invitation for you to reinvest in the basics of your Buddhist practice. That invitation includes direction regarding how Buddhism will help you with death and grief.

There is a practical aspect of death people can overlook. Death comes with paperwork. Part IV acknowledges the business of death. It is not a "how-to" guide with forms and checklists. It is a reminder that while you attend to the practical matters, you must also take care of yourself.

Along the way, you navigate how death impacts the people around you. And this is why Part V of Carpooling with Death includes plenty of discussion on how other people project their beliefs and opinions on you. Some people will baffle you, while others will pleasantly surprise you.

We conclude the journey in Part VI, with the acknowledgment that it is time for you to redesign your life. You are not the one who died, so live.

Your experiences will not be exactly like mine. Your stories will be different. The ways in which people are challenging and the ways in which people help you will vary as well. But when you have moments when you want to know what happened to someone else who has walked a similar path, when you wonder, "Is this normal?" "Am I going crazy?" or "What's wrong with me?", I hope that this is when I can help you.

I want you to have a friend, one who has taken this journey, too, and who understands what you are going through. This book is me reaching out to you, to be that friend.

"Just as a mother would protect her only child with her life, even so, let one cultivate a boundless love toward all beings.

"Let him radiate boundless love toward the entire world—above, below, and across—unhindered, without ill will, without enmity." – Sn 1.8

I cannot protect you from death. I do not want to protect you from death. Death is not something to be protected from—it is something to face with equanimity. Death is an integral part of life. Let's move forward now and do the work not just to confront death, but to accept death as your friend and companion.

I will be here with you. A mentor, someone who has walked with death, someone who can introduce you to my friend the Grim Reaper, someone who can help you establish your own happy and healthy relationship with him.

Thank you for coming along for the ride.

PART I

CARPOOLING WITH DEATH

Chapter 1

Learning to Carpool
with Death

It's a Thursday afternoon and, like so many others, I am stuck on a crowded Los Angeles freeway. Like the song says, just another crazy day in L.A. I know I am going to be late for my evening class. I also know that, in theory, I left with time to spare. There is no reason for me to be late. But unless teleporting becomes a reality within the next thirty minutes, I am not going to make it.

To my left, I see other cars whizzing by. The reward for not being a typical solo L.A. driver is the carpool lane. If there are two of you, you can use the carpool lane. And if you do, you avoid the type of mess that I am sitting in right now.

Suddenly, it occurs to me that I too could join the carpool lane. After all, I am not alone in the car. I look over to the passenger seat, and I see him. At least, I think the right pronoun is he. I have always assumed my current passenger to be a man. There he is, right next to me. Big, tall and boney, with that silly scythe and those over-the-top black robes. I am riding with death. As I glance over at him, he flashes me a skeletal smile.

For a moment I imagine it, me, in the carpool lane with Death. Actually, what I imagine is that moment when I get pulled over for driving solo in the carpool lane.

"But officer, I am not alone. I have Death right here with me." And that is when the call for backup would go out. "We have another crazy one who thinks her imaginary friend is with her, and guess what? She calls her invisible friend Death."

You see, nobody else can see my carpool buddy. But I know he's there.

Death does not seem to be bothered by the traffic, although I don't *know* because he hasn't spoken to me—yet. He has been with me quite a bit, but somehow I know that right now, he might be here *with* me, but he is not here *for* me. When the time comes, he is probably going to say something like, "NOW HUG YOUR WIFE GOODBYE," because he was here for my husband, Ed.

You would think I would be freaked out. The Grim Reaper does not exactly engender warm, fuzzy feelings. I can't say that I am completely at peace with the knowledge that the man I love is dying, but I don't sense any malevolence coming from my carpool partner. Just an unusual type of companionship. Death has always been with me, with all of us. Maybe you do not see him sitting next to you in the car, or walking with you in the aisles at Trader Joe's, but he's here. He always has been and he always will be.

You can ignore him, but he is never ignoring you. He knows you and everyone whom you love. And when it is time, he will come. Not out of spite or malice. He comes because it is his job to escort each of us to whatever comes next. As my dear father used to say during his final days, nobody gets out of this alive.

Welcome to carpooling with death. Come for a ride with us, me and my carpool buddy Grim. To become comfortable with his company is to become comfortable with the impermanence of life. You can expect to cry, and to laugh.

You will see that the Grim Reaper is not menacing or malevolent. He is not the one who decides when someone dies. He is the one who comes to deliver the news. Depending on what you believe, he is an escort. He is performing a service. He is a neutral party. When someone is suffering, with no hope of recovery, you are probably glad for his arrival.

Maybe you do not think it is possible to become comfortable with death, but that is exactly what this book will help you do. As you read about some of the experiences that death will bring your way, you will be able to see them all for what they truly are: just another part of life. But it is a part of life where having a friend and a guide makes all of the difference. Your friends and family might not be prepared to help you. And as you work with your emotions, and you see others around you struggle, you will probably ask yourself, "Is this normal?" and "Has this every happened to anyone else?" Yes, it is normal and yes, it has happened to others, too.

Between 2012 and 2017, I really got to know the Grim Reaper. He came for my father in 2012, then within a five-day period in 2014 he came back for mother and my husband. Not cool, Grim, not cool. I saw him again the next year with the loss of an old friend, and he popped by in 2016 for my favorite uncle, and then back again for my aunt in 2017. I am not whining or engaging in morbid bragging. Everything that happened to me will happen to everyone else. Others have lost more family members in an even shorter period of time. We will all experience death. There is no reason for you to do this alone.

For now, back to our carpool. Death may not be much of a conversationalist, but at least he does not tell you how to drive or demand that you listen to his favorite music. And that is pretty high praise for a carpool partner.

Chapter 2

Nobody Gets Out of This Alive

"Nobody gets out of this alive." This is what my father said when faced with his diagnosis of terminal lung cancer. He didn't coin the saying, but it fit the situation and his personality. I have to think that, when faced with his mortality, Dad must have had some complicated and conflicting thoughts. But with us, he was always steady. Always the stoic New Englander. He wanted to make sure that we understood that he was dying. Not in any dramatic, morbid sense. He just wanted to know that we were in tune with reality. If he could not live, he was going to try to help us face his death.

There was only one time when he indulged in a little bit of cynicism, and even that made sense. We had always shared a similar sense of humor. We loved puns, we enjoyed a dry wit and, once in a while, a hint of sarcasm. So when one of the nurses at the oncology center was reviewing his medications with him and asked him what they did for him, for just a brief moment, Dad looked at me, cracked a wry smile and said, so quietly that I think only I could hear him, "Apparently nothing." And truer words were never spoken. The blood pressure medication and the cholesterol medication did nothing to ward off the lung cancer.

Dad received his diagnosis in mid-May 2012. We had already been planning a visit for Memorial Day weekend. It turned out that this coincided with his first radiation treatment. He had a tumor on his back that was causing him quite a bit of discomfort. The radiation was not going to cure his cancer, but it could zap the tumor so that it relieved him of some of the pain.

I strongly objected when Dad said he would drive himself to radiation. I wanted to be there with him for whatever moments I could have. Ed agreed that we should go. So off we went. Mom hesitated and hung back. This was so hard for her. She was still processing it all in her way. I think Dad wanted to drive himself as a way of protecting her.

The oncology center was new and state-of-the-art. Mom and Dad lived in an area that was a hub for their region. People came to their town from all around for services, and this included medical care. At the time, it was one of the few places that had a specific type of radiation machine. The TrueBeam™ radiation machine could rotate around the body and deliver a much more accurate treatment than other methods, resulting in higher doses on the targeted spot and less burning and tissue damage to the surrounding area.

The oncology center team were warm and loving. They were happy to see family members in attendance. In fact, they *wanted* to see family members participating in the treatment process. We called home to Mom and let her know that we were not just sitting in the waiting room; this was a group participation event. She immediately got in the car and raced over.

The technician for the TrueBeam™ radiation machine invited us in and give us a tour. He showed us how the device worked, and how the beam rotated around the body. He let us stay while he worked to position Dad. He was enthusiastic about sharing his work and glad to see a family involved. But he knew the reality of Dad's cancer, and he knew that he was helping to alleviate pain, not working toward remission. We left the room when it was time for the actual treatment to begin. I was trying to be cheerful and nonchalant, tugging on Dad's toes as I walked past him, but I was fighting back my tears, and so was the technician.

Those radiation treatments did shrink the tumor and did quite a bit to reduce Dad's pain. One day, during a visit after his radiation treatments ended, Dad sat me down at his computer and asked me to show him how to create a decorative certificate using Word. I was a bit surprised because in the past he had made fun and silly certificates and sent them to me. "Best Daughter to Watch Godzilla With" was one of my favorites. I was his only daughter, but I took the win!

Later, I would realize that his point was to create the certificate together. To spend time on an activity that was part of his cancer, but not in a negative way. He wanted us to have a special and fun memory from this experience. Together we created a certificate for "Trudy," the name that he gave to the TrueBeam™ radiation machine. He gave one copy to me, and one to the team and the technician at the oncology center. They loved it. After Dad died, one of them approached me to let me know that they kept the certificate in the radiation room. It made everybody smile.

When my dad was in his final hours, and he could no longer speak to us, I told him over and over again what a good father he had been to me. How fortunate I was. And I told him that he had done such a good job during his illness. And I meant it.

In the Dhammapada, a collection of sayings attributed to the Buddha, is this verse:

Some do not understand
that we must die,
But those who do realize this
settle their quarrels.
Dhp 6

I would not have envisioned my father as someone with quarrels to settle. But with an understanding that he would die, Dad made sure that I would not wonder about his love for me or wonder about what he really thought about me and my life choices.

On a phone call a few years before his cancer diagnosis, Dad became very serious and told me that he always wanted me to know that he loved me and was proud of me. That there was nothing I had done that he was upset over. It was an important and difficult and liberating conversation. Important and difficult because together we were acknowledging out loud that his death would come; liberating because it removed any hint of guilt or thought of parental disapproval. Not that I doubted my father's love for me, and I was not ashamed of my life choices. But to be a Buddhist when my parents were staunch Catholics was initially not an easy choice. To divorce my first husband when my parents were staunch Catholics was not an easy decision. In that phone call, Dad made sure I did not have to wonder about his support for me. And that was quite the gift.

Even before he knew he had terminal cancer, Dad was becoming a death coach. When he received his diagnosis, so much of his behavior was a lesson in how to navigate your final days with grace and ease.

Aside from reminding us that "Nobody gets out of this alive," he would also say, "I don't wonder why me, I know the answer is, 'why *not* me.'" He was not going to spend precious time raging against death or thinking he was getting a raw deal. He was going to spend time loving Mom and being with his friends and family. He had a clear set of priorities. For example, on one weekend visit, he announced that he had called and rescheduled his radiation appointment for another day. Today, he was feeling good, and he wanted us all to go on a road trip. For a brief moment, I wondered whether or not that was a good idea. Before I could say anything, Dad just gave me a look. In that look, he helped me see his perspective. He was going to die. The radiation was not a cure. It alleviated some discomfort. The appointment could wait. We were here now, and he felt well enough to go on an outing. That was the right answer. He wanted to create happy memories for us.

During the six months between his diagnosis and his death, we celebrated Father's Day, Mom's birthday, my birthday, Dad's birthday and Ed's birthday. Just two and a half weeks before he died, Dad celebrated Oktoberfest with friends, enjoying beer and bratwurst.

When Dad died, Ed was devasted. I know that he remained calm and quiet for me, but he lost a friend and a father figure and one of his favorite people. Ed did not take a liking to many people. He did not enjoy talking to many people. But he loved spending time with Dad. And the feeling was mutual. On so many occasions, Mom and I would walk along together, only to stop and wonder "Where are the boys?"

The boys would be far behind us, stopped and engaged in animated conversation.

I know that as Ed went through his illness, he used my father as a mentor. He would say, "Dad did it, I can do this, too." Or he would say, "When I don't know what do or say, I think about your dad and I try to be like him." In this way, Dad helped me through two deaths. For that, I will always be grateful.

Almost two years to the day later, my husband Ed would follow a similar path. Dad died on November 19, 2012, and Ed followed him on November 25, 2014. They died from the same type of lung cancer.

Chapter 3

Bittersweet Goodbyes

Just as I knew it would, the time came to say goodbye to my loved ones. I cannot say that I was 100% ready, but I was 100% aware of death. I was not going to be surprised. I was going to be as involved in the process as each death would allow me to be.

Dad

Ed hated to travel during Thanksgiving week. In fact, he had laid down the law and stated that we would never travel during Thanksgiving week. He was not a "lay down the law" kind of guy, so when he made this kind of proclamation, it usually made me giggle. But I also worked to honor his request. Although this specific request sometimes disappointed our family and friends, it did, in fact, make our Thanksgivings so much more enjoyable. We typically stayed home and enjoyed our quiet time together. We had a Honey-baked ham for him, and stuffing and sweet potatoes and green bean casserole for me. I baked him an apple pie, and when I was feeling energetic, sometimes I would bake a pumpkin pie for myself.

This year was no different, except that my father had terminal lung cancer. Back in May, he had been given six weeks to live. Thanks to his tenacity and a drug called Tarceva, we had been granted more time than the oncologist thought was possible.

Once Dad was diagnosed, Ed and I began to visit on a monthly basis. Of course, my initial response was to move up to Sequim, Washington, where Mom and Dad lived, and stay for the duration. After discussing the situation with my parents, we settled on regular visits of four to five days each month. Mom and Dad had a strong circle of supportive friends, and Sequim was a hub on the Olympic Peninsula, with plenty of good medical care.

When we discussed our November visit, we all agreed that we would not come for Thanksgiving, we would come the weekend before. Mom and Dad had a tradition of hosting Thanksgiving for their group, and there was no strong urge that we had to spend this last Thanksgiving together.

Two days before we were to arrive, Mom called me. She said that Dad was in the hospital and it did not look good. She told me he would probably still be in the hospital when we arrived. The next morning, the prognosis was the same. We tried to schedule an earlier flight, but could not. The doctor said that it was now a matter of time. Maybe a couple of weeks, but more likely days. Mom told me that each time Dad woke up he asked if Ed and I had arrived yet.

The day that we arrived, Dad was having a good day. He was still in the hospital, and he and Mom were arranging for his home hospice care. He told the staff to wait and bring his lunch when Ed and I arrived so that we could all have lunch together.

When we arrived, it was clear that the cancer was taking over. But we had lunch together, and we talked. He teased me about not knowing the west wing of the hospital from the east wing. Which was true. I was and still am directionally impaired.

He sent Mom home ahead of him to wait for the hospice team to set up the hospital bed and the other assorted equipment. After she was gone, he informed me that she had decided she would not move away from Sequim. She wanted to stay in the house. This was disconcerting because they had both always said that whoever was left behind wanted to come and live in Southern California, near me. But Mom was independent. I understood her not wanting to leave her friends and her community. I assured Dad that we would keep coming to visit, just as we had been doing during his illness. He expressed concern about her finances, and our ability to afford to keep visiting, and I assured him that everything would be fine. We could afford to keep visiting indefinitely, and if Mom needed any financial support, we would help with that, too.

Later that day, while we were waiting for the ambulance to transport Dad back home, he looked at me, and he asked me to call Mom and see how things were progressing. After I made the call, he looked at me and smiled and said, "I just wanted to make sure that your mother made it home OK."

That thoughtfulness would permeate his final days. We brought him home on Friday at around 5 pm, and he passed on Monday just before noon. On Saturday morning, he asked Mom and me to make him breakfast while he chatted with Ed, giving each of us something to do, a memory to have from his final moments.

In the evening, when it was my turn to watch over him and administer his medication, sometimes I would talk and tell him how much I loved and respected him. Other times I would meditate. While he was no longer speaking, I could swear that when I would touch him and meditate, he would breathe in and out with me. And when I gave him his medication, he would incline his head toward me, ever so slightly, making it easier to administer his morphine drops.

When he left us, it was about twenty minutes after the priest had performed the anointing of the sick. Ed and I were out of the room. Mom called us in to let us know that he had taken his last breath. Later she would apologize, saying that she knew he was almost gone and that she wanted to be alone with him. We both assured her that we understood and that this was their moment.

Two years later, Ed and I would have our own final moment.

Ed

Final Moments
(A Haiku)

He came back to me.
And three of us embraced,
me, my love and death.

"NOW HUG YOUR WIFE GOODBYE."

I imagine those were the instructions that Death gave to Ed, as he came to escort him away.

Ed and I had shared a love of the Discworld novels by Terry Pratchett. In Discworld, Death is a character. In fact, there are two books in the series where Death takes a leading role:, Mort and Reaper Man. You always know when Death is in the scene because he speaks in all capitals.

And Ed was able to sit up and give me one last hug just before died.

I did not know that this was his last day. I knew it was coming. I knew it would be within the next few days. But until he sat up and hugged me, and then died on his way back to the pillow, I did not know this was the day.

As with many people who go through a terminal illness, he had an energy surge a few days before he died. He got feisty with me for having some outside help come in. Then he gave me flowers and a card as a way of apologizing for his tantrum. We went out and found him something fun to eat. He went off for cheeseburgers and to visit a local Buddhist temple with his best friend.

When he returned from his day out with his friend, he looked at me, and he said, "We need to call the hospice nurse to come., I am having a problem." That was early Saturday evening, and that started his journey toward his final moments.

The nurse arrived and was unable to perform the necessary procedure. He needed to have a catheter inserted and for some reason, she was unable to insert the catheter. She called for back up, and the results were the same. We were told to go to the emergency room. In the emergency room, the nurses were similarly unable to assist. We waited for a specialist to be called in.

It was during this time that Ed's story and Mom's story intersect. The last time I had spoken to Mom was Thursday evening. We had laughed, and we cried a bit. She told me that I was her best friend. She told me about a party that she was going to on Saturday.

I was surprised when I called her on Friday, and she did not return my call. We spoke every day. If we missed one another, we always left messages. When I called on Saturday and received her answering machine again, my intuition was bouncing off the charts.

While Ed and I were waiting for the specialist, I looked down and noticed that someone had been trying to call me. I did not recognize the phone number, but I knew the area code. And I saw that there was a message. My heart sank. I listened to the message and sank to the floor. Two of my mother's friends were at her house. She was not opening the door, she was not answering the phone, and she had not shown up for the party earlier that day. Mom would never voluntarily miss a social event.

I returned the call. At this point, the friends had already called the sheriff. He asked for my permission to break in and, of course, I granted it. We all knew what he would find. Mom had died peacefully while sitting on the couch, reading her prayer book. In fact, she had most likely died within a couple of hours of our last phone call.

At this point, some of the emergency room staff came to check on me, to see what was wrong. Of course, they assumed it was something with Ed. When I told them that now along with navigating the final days of Ed's terminal cancer, I was giving directions long distance on where to send my mother's body, it was more than some of them could handle. One of the nurses left the room with tears in his eyes and never came back.

I don't know if Ed ever fully understood that Mom had died. The emergency room staff gave him some very strong pain meds. Eventually, the specialist arrived and inserted the catheter. We returned home. Ed never regained his strength.

When it became apparent that we were heading into the final days, I arranged to have him moved to a hospital bed. The hospice nurse who had helped us on Friday came on Monday and was shocked to see his decline.

He died on Tuesday. He started the day groggy and disoriented, but able to speak. As the day progressed, his condition deteriorated. I became busy with him and forgot to cancel the appointment with the hospice-provided reiki master. It turns out, this was a good thing. When she arrived, she immediately grasped the situation. While the hospice nurse who was there was not being helpful or responsive to my requests, the reiki master jumped in and began giving the hospice nurse directions. Later I would learn that the reiki master had her own experience with helping a family member die and that was how she knew what was going on and what to do.

Eventually, Ed became less agitated and rested. His best friend stopped by to be with both of us. Once Ed and I were alone, I began to chant to him in P li. I chanted some basic Buddhist texts. I kept repeating them; I suppose it was soothing to both of us.

Suddenly his eyes flew open, and he looked at me. And he lurched forward and threw his arms around my neck. And then, just as quickly, he was gone. I felt him die.

In his final hug, he gave me the most beautiful gift. He used his remaining energy to let me know how much he loved me.

PART II

LIVING WITH DEATH

Chapter 4

Overcoming the Fear

Now that I have been able to share the stories of my loved ones, it is time to move forward, to discuss the specifics of what it is like to live with death as your companion. It is my fondest wish that the experiences and challenges I faced around being afraid of death and learning to live the best life possible while grappling with death will assist you and inspire you so that you have many moments of peace and happiness throughout your journey.

"Mommy, she can't see. Bonnie Muffin Speckleberry cannot see. Look at how she keeps bumping into things."

Bonnie Muffin Speckleberry was our dog, a cute little Maltese puppy who was not even a year old. Her name was just Bonnie. For some reason, I felt this was incomplete. If I had a first name, a middle name and a last name, then so should our dog. Bonnie had just come home from the veterinarian's office, with a clean bill of health, but she was not OK. Soon my parents would have to make the difficult decision to have her put to sleep. I remember crying myself to sleep.

Somewhere along the way, I developed a fear of death. Not *my* death, but the death of the people and the animals I loved. I became conscious of the fact that we would all die, and that meant that the day would come when I would have to say goodbye to my parents. When I married Ed, who was fifteen years my senior, it became likely that I would outlive him, too. There were times when I thought that perhaps I would get lucky and I would die first. But I never wanted my parents to have that experience. And because I knew how much Ed loved me, I never wanted him to have that experience, either.

Depending on who your teachers are and who you sit with, becoming a Buddhist can be like training for death. If you follow the lesson on impermanence all the way to its natural conclusion, it is not just your thoughts and emotions that are rising and falling. Everything is rising and falling. Every one of us rises and ultimately falls.

You would do well to spend time considering death. Thinking that this could be your last day. That this could be the last day of someone you love. The purpose of this is not to dwell in a place of morbidity, but to appreciate the preciousness of the life that you have been given. To be born as a human being is a gift. In this lifetime, you are able to practice the dharma. When you die, you might lose this opportunity.

It is not just good times and bad times that will pass; we will, too. It is useful to work with the phrase, "We too shall pass." "I too shall pass;" "Mom and Dad too shall pass;" "Ed too shall pass."

I came to realize that what I really feared was being left behind by the people I loved, being without them. I also began to understand that spending time being afraid that this would happen was of no use. It was going to happen. I did not know when or who would die first, but I was not facing uncertainty.

Slowly, I began to allow myself to think about the deaths of my loved ones. Instead of chasing these thoughts away, I learned to welcome them. To meditate on the death of my father was to help me experience his death in advance. This meditation was a way of preparing me for the deep sadness I would feel when he really did die. I came to a point where I became comfortable accepting that the people I loved would die, and that it would be difficult, but that I would be able to face it.

People are going to die. This is beyond your control. To be in a constant state of agitation over this truth will only ruin the time that you have. Denial will just make the moment of their deaths more difficult. It is better for you to live with the knowledge and understanding that death will come. It will be difficult, but you will be OK. Love your friends and family, and enjoy your time with them while they are here.

There is, in fact, nothing to fear, because death is coming. There is no reason for you to live in fear of something that is a certainty. Live in acceptance of that certainty and prepare yourself. Of course, this is easier said than done.

It was Always Going to Be Cancer

Ed's father died from a massive heart attack while walking with Ed to the store in Brooklyn, New York. Ed was just past his thirteenth birthday, and his father was fifty-two. Most of his father's family died from heart disease when they were in their fifties or early sixties.

Based on his experience with his father, Ed had a self-imposed expiration date of fifty-two years. In fact, when we first started dating, he tried to scare me away. He was convinced that he only had two years left to live. Once he had made it past his fifty-second birthday, I wanted to believe that one day, when he was in his mid-eighties or beyond, he would die in his sleep from a heart attack. Leaving me as a widow, somewhere in my seventies at a point in life where I could keep busy with friends and travel and volunteering until it was my turn to die.

The problem was that long before Ed became ill, I had already had an insight. I felt that somehow, even though he was technically healthy, I did not think that he would live past the age of seventy. Meaning that I would not make it to my sixties before becoming a widow. So much for the thought that I could keep busy and hang out waiting for death.

That insight was followed a few years later by another revelation. Ed was not going to die from a heart attack. It was going to be cancer. This was probably not particularly intuitive of me. When you begin to have cancer scares, you start to understand that there is a high likelihood that one of those scares will be real.

At that time, we were waiting for results from his second prostate cancer scare. When we had his first scare, the doctor told him that he almost certainly had prostate cancer. He had never seen someone with a PSA count so high without cancer being the issue. And yet, somehow,

Ed was the one. He managed to have a freakishly high PSA count and no cancer. He had a severe infection. After a couple of weeks on antibiotics, he was good to go. Then it happened again. And yes, during his second prostate cancer scare, he was cleared of cancer and once again diagnosed with an infection. After a course of antibiotics, his PSA count returned to normal. And for a while, so did our life together.

It was at this point that somehow I knew that whether or not this time it was cancer, there was more cancer in our future. Eventually, we moved on to our next scare, a small white spot in his mouth. The spot was cancer. It was removed, he went back for regular check-ups and he received a clean bill of health.

Then one day, during his regular physical, when the doctor said stick out your tongue, there it was—again. A white spot. More than a spot, he had a tumor growing on his tongue. This time it was much more severe, and its removal was painful.

And at the post-operative checkup, we were told:

"It's all clear. I removed all of the cancer, and there is no indication that it has spread."

That is what I reported to all who asked, even though, in my heart, I could feel that it was not right. When people asked, I lied. I lied to myself, and I lied to them, and I lied for him. Most people were happy to take what I said at face value. It was good news, it was hopeful news, and most people do not know how to deal with difficult news. Nor do they want to deal with difficult news. And if you tell them that even though the doctor said everything is going to be OK, you know otherwise, they will accuse you of being negative or inviting drama. Or, worse yet, they will misrepresent the law of attraction to you and tell you that you are inviting cancer with your negative thoughts.

"There is so much cancer in my family that I assume that one day I will die from it too."

That's what an acquaintance of mine said after she asked me about Ed and his prognosis. She had just told me that she could see how close we were and how his cancer had impacted us significantly. And she had asked me about his prognosis. I answered her with the words that we had heard from his oncologist:

"All of the cancer has been removed, and there is no reason to believe there will be any additional issues."

Once again, I was speaking rehearsed false words. As I spoke the words, they rang false to me, and I could see on her face as she turned away from me that she felt it, too.

When you love someone, and you are together every day, you go back and forth between seeing what you want and seeing how things are. At least, that is how it was for me. I wanted the doctor to be right, but I could also see that Ed was not well.

It had been just two years since my father had received his cancer diagnosis. In fact, the timeline was almost the same. The difference was that with Dad we knew it was lung cancer. It would be a couple of more months before we learned that Ed had the same small-cell lung carcinoma. And there was something about that timeline that felt all too familiar.

In August, the lung cancer diagnosis came, and after a brief attempt at chemotherapy, cancer won. We went into hospice the end of October, and on November 25, he died. Two years and six days after Dad, and five days after Mom.

Chapter 5

Ready or Not, Death Will Come

A friend's mother was diagnosed with lung cancer and it was deemed too far along to be curable. Together, they discussed hospice care. Then, unexpectedly, her mother had a massive stroke and died in her sleep. This was quite a shock. My friend was just coming to terms with losing her mother, and then death stepped in and took over.

Many of us see illness through a natural progression. From diagnosis, to treatment plans, to treatments. The good news is that there are many, many cancer survivors, and on their journey, some of them learn to make friends with death.

When chemotherapy and radiation and other treatments do not work, or the cancer or disease is too advanced, then together you enter the world of the terminally ill. At first, your loved one may not need special care. My father went for months living a somewhat normal life. Which is why, in his own way, he worked to remind us that nobody gets out of this alive.

It is important to discuss the logistics of death. Perhaps your loved one will go in his or her sleep, before you need to consider hospice or palliative care. In a perfect world, you would have these conversations BEFORE either of you is ill. You might discuss this while you create your will or your trust. You might discuss it when family members or friends are facing their own deaths. Maybe you talk about it after a funeral or memorial service.

Our first conversations about death occurred after September 11, 2001. We were beginning to travel quite a bit. In fact, in spring 2002, we were going to go to Italy and France. Ed broached the subject to me. He wondered out loud what would happen to our house, to our cats, if we both died. This prompted us to create our wills and to have discussions about "do not resuscitate" orders and who should take care of our physical stuff. We knew that we had no strong attachment to any kind of religious service. We spoke a little bit about if one of us became ill, but at this point, our thought process was really about dying together in a terrorist attack.

As Ed's mother aged, she made sure that we understood what she did and did not want. She had already arranged her burial at a reputable Jewish cemetery. She wanted a small service with a Rabbi presiding. She too had a "do not resuscitate." Ed was her primary resource and I was her secondary. Discussing her plans encouraged us to reconfirm our plans.

When my father became terminally ill, we became even more clear. At least, Ed did. Like my father, if or when it became necessary, he wanted to die at home. Me, I was not so sure. I felt like I would prefer to be in a hospital or other facility so that my friends and family would not have to deal with the hands-on requirements of taking care of the dying.

Each of our deaths is very personal. You can say that it is the most personal of our experiences. Whenever possible, it is important to give your loved ones the death they request.

My father wanted to die at home. My husband wanted to die at home. My uncle preferred the hospital, surrounded by family and friends.

After my father died, my mother repeatedly said, "I'm leaving this house feet first!" The plans that she and Dad had made were that whoever was widowed would move to California, near me. Not necessarily to live with me, but to be near me. The idea was that it was too difficult to expect me to move to Washington State. That plan, however, never came to pass.

Mom was very independent. After Dad died, it took her a while to understand that nobody was trying to make her move. During one of our early phone calls, she said, "I suppose now you are calling me every day to make sure that I am still alive!" Well no, I was calling her every day because she was an extreme extrovert and Dad, the introvert, had been her dedicated listener. I knew that she needed to talk. Eventually she understood, and we entered into a wonderful friendship.

When Death Moves In

When it came time for Dad to be in hospice, it happened rather quickly. One day he was fine, the next day he was admitted to the hospital, and two days later, on a Friday afternoon, he returned to the house and we began home hospice. We had a hospital bed set up for him in the living room, and we took turns sitting with him throughout the night. He died that Monday.

You may or may not work with a hospice organization, and you might not want to think about hospice at all. But the best time to think about it is in advance. To do so is not engaging in negativity. It is preparedness.

The organization that my parents selected came highly recommended. Although we only worked with them for a few days, they were terrific. These were nurses and other caretakers who were helping out on a volunteer basis. They could not have been more loving or more professional. They had a helpline to call for questions or concerns or for when conditions changed. They came by about twice a day. When Dad died, it was just moments before one of the hospice team arrived. She knew what to do and how to take care of us.

With Ed, home hospice was a completely different experience. The service we used came highly recommended by his physician. It was not a volunteer organization. It was a paid healthcare service provider. Part of the difference in our experience was because Ed was in hospice for about a month, while Dad was in hospice for less than a week. But a more significant aspect of it had to do with the attitudes of the care staff.

Sometimes it seemed like they were most concerned with filling out forms and checklists and following procedures. All of those things are important and are required for them to keep their licensing, but there were days when I wondered if there were any human beings behind the clipboards.

The night that Ed died, the nurse on call could barely bring herself to come back to the house. I had to remind her that it was her job to confirm his death. And when she half-heartedly offered to stay with me until the mortuary arrived, I immediately told her she was free to go. The relief on her face was palpable.

This is an area where we could have done a better job. If together we had sat down and had more thorough conversation about home hospice, perhaps we might have preselected an organization that would have been as compassionate as the volunteer group we worked with for my father.

Because the team who helped with Dad was so good, I think we assumed that would be our experience, too. If you feel that home hospice might be in your future, research your options in advance. We trusted Ed's primary care physician to make a recommendation. I am sure she thought she was connecting us with an excellent service, but I would never recommend that service to others.

You have choices when it comes to hospice. Ask your friends and family for recommendations. If you have friends who are in the medical profession, get their opinions. If you know others whose family has been in hospice, seek them out. Your priest, pastor or other spiritual leader or your spiritual community might also have some tips for you. In the United States, there is the National Hospice and Palliative Care (NHPCO) Organization, a nonprofit representing hospice and palliative care organizations. Their mission is to improve end-of-life care and expand access to hospice care. They are a helpful source and even provide information on what you need to think about as you consider the various hospice organizations available to you. NHPCO has a checklist that you can use to help make a more informed choice. These people come into your home, and you want to know what type of training they have, and what kind of screening occurs before someone is allowed to provide care. You want to know whether or not you will receive twenty-four-hour support and how many patients each case-worker supports at one time. You might also want to know if the hospice provides support services for family members, such as counseling or access to a chaplain.

Even though the company we worked with was less than stellar, dying at home was the right choice for Ed. Ed was not aware of most of the issues with the hospice team, and that is how it should have been. He needed to be in peace at home, and if you or your loved one wishes to die at home, find a way to make it as loving and peaceful as possible.

Chapter 6

It's OK to Laugh

It is OK to laugh. It is OK to find humor in death and dying. Those moments of dark humor are what let you know that you are still alive. Those moments of dark humor relieve some of the stress and tension and bring you hope. You will have plenty of days to cry.

Death is not all doom and gloom. You can have some beautiful moments during the dying process. There is nothing like death to help point out the absurdity of life and the foolishness with which we cling to life and to our beliefs and positions.

When the hospice team started coming to the house, I learned that baby wipes are a critical item. I had no idea. They are almost as versatile as duct tape. I think every care worker who came to the house asked me where I kept the baby wipes. I began to have fun with this, by tracking how long they were in the house before they asked me for them. I think the shortest time was about two minutes.

As a woman with no children or grandchildren, I had no baby wipes. Apparently, my lack of baby wipes was astounding. They would tell me, "You need to buy some baby wipes and have them on hand."

I wanted to say to them, "Really? I am way past the baby stage in life, why do you think I should have baby wipes? And by the way, I am busy helping my husband through the end of his life, why do you think baby wipes should even make my priority list?" Eventually, I replied with, "If they are a supply you need, why don't you ask your employer to make them part of your kit?" As long as they were visiting the house, the requests for baby wipes never stopped. And because I was not in tune with buying baby wipes, their requests for baby wipes were never met. However, I am confident that Ed's death was not caused by a lack of baby wipes.

A few years before Ed became ill, he had some other health issues. These issues led him to need a catheter for several days. It was uncomfortable for him. And, to be blunt, it was messy. While I was on board for in sickness and in health, and I did not think that I was squeamish, I did not enjoy dealing with the catheter. It leaked. Sometimes it leaked while he was sleeping. Sometimes I was the first one to know that it was leaking. I think I can leave the rest to your imagination.

Long before Ed and the catheter, there was our cat Alex. Alexis Theodora Kitty, AKA Alex the Kitty. Alex came to us as a stray. She wrangled her way into our hearts. OK, she wrangled her way into my heart and, with resignation, Ed accepted her. Alex came with a problem, a very unpleasant issue. That issue was pee. To be formal about it, inappropriate urination.

Alex seemed to go by the credo, "Why use the litter box when I can pee on this shirt, or this towel, or this pillow, or this piece of paper, or Margaret's leg while she is taking a nap?" Yes, she did pee on me once while I was napping. We considered changing her name to Peabody.

During the final month of Ed's cancer, he began to have issues with urination. And so at a time when Alex had mastered her problems and was using the litter box, Ed could not use his litter box. Unfortunately, he once again required a catheter.

So here we were again, back to dealing with pee. One day, Ed looked at me with a mischievous glint in his eye and said, "Well, at least I know you won't take me to the pound. You dealt with Alex's pee; now you can deal with mine." I could not help but laugh. We even joked about whether or not he should drip on Alex's blanket in retribution for all of the times that she used his shirts or pants as her private bathroom.

The day after Ed died, when it was time for me to go to the mortuary to arrange for Ed's cremation, I recall texting back and forth with my best friend:

She texted me: "I will follow you to the mortuary."

I replied: "Don't follow too closely. I may jump into the oven."

Her response: "Then I will pull you out."

Me: "Better bring your oven mitts."

And so it goes, you laugh, you cry, and you surprise yourself with how some days it all feels so normal. Which is perfect, because death is normal.

Chapter 7

Design YOUR Days

When you have lived with someone for many years, you think you know them. Once in a while, though, he will surprise you. To live with that person while he is terminally ill is to live with the man you know and yet also to meet different versions of that same man.

What a lesson in impermanence it is!

Some days I would see the man I thought I knew, the man I married. Other days, I would see someone who looked like him and who had the same voice, but I was not sure who was in there.

There was the man who reminded me that even though he called me "his rock," I did not always have to be strong, I did not have to take care of everything. It would be OK for me to have a breakdown.

But there was also the man who had a temper tantrum because when I was at my breaking point, I began to bring in help. I started to have more care workers come. He was angry that I would allow outsiders into our private life. He threatened to leave me. The next day, that same man sent me flowers to apologize and to let me know how much he loved me.

And there was the man who understood that he was dying, so he no longer needed to care about high cholesterol and other dietary concerns. Every day, he would come up with something fun to eat. Each day, he came up with a new version of his last meal.

It was so joyful to watch him consider his possibilities and then to name his selection. I think sometimes he knew early in the day what he wanted, but he would keep me in suspense until it was time to do something about it. And then we would set out on a fun food adventure.

He worked his way through his cravings like a hungry teenager: Chinese spare ribs, hamburgers, bacon everything, plates of pasta, fried chicken, and pastrami sandwiches. He kept this up until about three days before he died.

My father also used his time to create memories with us. One day while we were visiting, he made a surprise announcement that he felt like taking a road trip, under the condition that Ed and I shared the driving. And off we went to a location where he and Mom used to go on their own, and where we had all been on previous outings, too. To our good fortune, it was a beautiful day. We all enjoyed a nice lunch, then Mom and Dad sat on the restaurant patio and played cards while Ed and I walked along the nature trail.

During another visit, Dad asked me to help him make an award certificate for some of his medical team. He wanted to create a fun certificate to let them know how much he appreciated their help. It gave us some time to work together on something, and then together we drove to the oncology center and presented it. The team loved it! They put it up on the wall, in a place where everyone, staff and visitors alike, could see it.

The morning after we brought Dad home from the hospital and officially entered hospice, he asked Mom and me to make him breakfast. He did not want much, just a poached egg, some toast and coffee. Mom was in charge of the egg and the toast and I was in charge of the coffee. Dad then turned to Ed and asked him to help him out with a small issue on his computer. I do not think he was really hungry and I do not think he really needed to use his computer. He just wanted to give us all a little something to do. A way in which to interact with him. Later that day, he would begin to become unresponsive. But just before he did, he woke up. He looked at my mom, took her hand and said, "Are you OK?"

Dad and Ed used their final time and energy to create positive experiences and memories for themselves and those they loved.

Chapter 8

Create a Good Death

When it comes time for death, welcome that, too. Do not let anyone make you feel bad if you express that it is time.

A friend said to me, "He went so fast. It is too bad that he went so fast. It seems like you two just went into hospice mode."

"Yes," I replied, "but sometimes faster is better."

To which my friend replied, "But I am sure you wanted as much time with him as possible."

"He was starting to suffer. He was at a point where he was never going to get better. It is good that he is at peace."

Insistently my friend replied, "But you did not want him to die. I am sure you wish that he was still alive."

At this point, I changed the subject. We had different opinions about what it meant for it to be someone's time to die. For me to try to explain this would probably only result in this person thinking that I wanted my husband to die.

Knowing that he could not live, what I wanted was for him to have a good death. Not in a fatalistic way, but to live knowing that death is coming and to stop raging against it. If there are medical treatments that make sense, by all means, try them.

For Dad, as the doctor was examining him and they began to say that it was time for hospice, the doctor did mention some procedures. None of these procedures were going to cure his cancer or place him in remission. Maybe they would buy him some extra time. One of the potential procedures was going to be painful. Dad and Mom discussed all of this, and together they decided it was time to let go and let death come as it would come. I believe that this was very graceful and dignified.

With Ed, it became clear that the chemotherapy was not working, that the cancer had broken through. He too chose to let death come as it would come.

When it is time, work with your loved one to give him or her a good death. This does not mean that you do not cry and that you deny your sad feelings. But try to avoid fighting it. Avoid clinging to them and saying things like, "Don't leave me, you can't leave me, what am I going to do?" This only makes it harder for them to have a peaceful death. He or she is going to die anyway; try to make the process as calm and loving as possible.

Part of a good death is the ability to make the most of life, right up until your final moments together.

Death is a very personal matter. Like snowflakes or fingerprints, no two are exactly the same.

Both Dad and Ed wanted to die at home. Dad was fine with the hospital bed being set up in a space between the family room and the dining room. This way he was in the center of the activity. His time in official at-home hospice was short. He came home from the hospital on Friday and died on Monday.

Ed hated the idea of a hospital bed. In fact, he died a within a few hours of being moved to the hospital bed. He was just not going to have it. He did not want many visitors and, in fact, did not want anyone but me to help him. He begrudgingly accepted help from the hospice staff. He also was in hospice care for a month.

Mom, whose final moments I did not observe, also had the death she wanted. She stated over and over again, "I am leaving this house feet first." And that she did. She died of a heart attack, at the end of the day, sitting on the couch, reading her prayers. Just that day she had worked in her beloved garden. She was active right up until her final moment.

When you can, help your loved ones die their way. Really listen to what they want. Even if what they want is not what you want.

If being with someone who is sick or dying is difficult for you, consider which difficulty you would rather face:

> Pushing yourself to do something that is tough for you, but helps your loved one have a peaceful exit.

> Or

> Doing what is easy for you, and living with the knowledge that you could have helped someone you love one last time, but you didn't.

As much as I miss my loved ones, I never regret being with them during their final moments. If I had to do it again, I would. And for my loved ones who are still here, if I am able to be with them during their final moments, I will.

What makes it possible for me to continue to be with death? For me, it is my Buddhist practice.

PART III

DEATH IS PART OF YOUR PRACTICE

Chapter 9

It Helps to Have Faith

Last year, a friend of mine lost his grandmother. This was not his first experience with death, but it was his most difficult. They had a strong bond and enjoyed spending time together. Her absence left a hole in his life and in his heart. He also recognized that he did not have any clear beliefs around what happens after death. His religious education had not included discussions on death and the afterlife.

This confusion only made his grief more intense.

In facing his death, my father relied heavily upon his Catholicism. While Dad never forced his beliefs on me, he would occasionally discuss how his faith was helping him. He let me know that his faith enabled him to be accepting of his diagnosis and to be unafraid of death.

His church community helped him remain mentally strong as his time drew near. He and Mom had a family friend, a priest named Father Mark. Father Mark made regular visits to pray with them. He agreed to hold small prayer sessions with them and their friends. Mom, always the ultimate hostess, would turn these into prayers and breakfast, where of course she would prepare something amazing. As a group, they had spent many occasions enjoying Mom's cooking and hospitality, and this gave them all a continued sense of friendship and connection.

It was not just the community that helped my parents. It was their unwavering faith. They had a rock-solid foundation. They believed in God, and they believed in Jesus as their savior. They both believed that immediately after death the soul would be separated from the body and be judged. There was no reason for either of them to think that they would not be sent to heaven as a reward for their time here on earth. They also believed that one day there would be a final judgment day. A day when Jesus would return to earth. Just prior to this final judgment, their souls will be reunited with their bodies. During the final judgment, God, through his son Jesus, will make known his final word on all of history. Perhaps most importantly to my parents, they believed that they would be joined together again in eternity.

As Mom became more fully aware that Dad was in his final moments, she would say to him over and over again, "It's OK to go. I know you love me. The kids will take care of me until it is time for me to join you. We will be together again."

I am so glad that their Catholicism helped Mom and Dad. Likewise, I do not know how I could have made this journey without Buddhism. To be a Buddhist is to understand the Four Noble Truths and to seek to follow the Noble Eightfold Path. The first part of that path is right view: to accept that there is suffering, and that clinging to that which is impermanent causes suffering. Everyone and everything is impermanent.

When I was a new Buddhist, I thought that Buddhism only required logical thought and analysis. I thought that focused meditations were all I needed. It was with this mindset that I first encountered the Four Noble Truths:

1. There is stress and suffering, or *dukkha*. Another way to think of this is that in life, we have much dissatisfaction.
2. We experience this dissatisfaction because we become attached to either wanting good things to stay the same, or for difficult things to stop being difficult.
3. There is a way out of this dissatisfaction.
4. The way out of this dissatisfaction is to live your life in accordance with the Noble Eightfold Path.

Initially, I was stuck at number one. The way it was verbalized to me was, "Life is suffering." Immediately I rejected the notion that life is suffering. I had a happy life. I didn't have a depressed or unhappy bone in my body. Then I heard someone else teach. This time, the message was that *dukkha*, which can be translated as suffering, might also be translated as dissatisfaction or dis-ease. We strive for better jobs or fancier cars or larger homes. We cling to what we have. We try to avoid what we view as unpleasant. We do not want to be sick or experience anything unpleasant. This is what creates *dukkha*. Ah, now that made sense. Like others, I did spend time and energy in my life wanting to move to "the next level," and trying to avoid discomfort.

As I observed my experiences, I fully accepted the truth of dissatisfaction. But no faith was required for me to accept this truth. It came from direct experience.

The good news and the bad news was that the things I perceived as undesirable would not last forever, but then neither would the things I perceived as desirable.

There was a time when I was interviewing for a managerial position at a small organization. As part of their hiring process, they required me to have a physical at a local medical clinic. As part of the exam, the doctor asked me all kinds of questions about my current condition. I expressed to him that I was very fortunate. I was active and healthy and did not have any issues. Without missing a beat, he looked at me and said, "Well, that will change." That's impermanence!

You cannot fully embrace impermanence without embracing death. The way to embrace death is not to ignore it or deny it; it is to make it part of your life, to understand that it is your karma that determines what will happen to you. Your karma is made up of your past actions and your current actions. Nobody can tell you exactly what will happen to you and when it will happen.

Not knowing what will come, but knowing that whatever happens is part of your karma, is less stressful than worrying about what is coming. You cannot undo your past, so you do not need to worry about your past. Do good things now. There is no need to rush through any part of your life; it is all as it is meant to be.

Developing an understanding of suffering, karma and impermanence allowed me to accept death. I never asked, "Why does Dad have to die?" Or, "Why does Ed have to die?" Or, "Why did Mom die?" I knew that all of us are subject to old age, illness and death. I would read this passage frequently during Dad's illness and then again during Ed's illness.

"Those who have come to be,
those who will be:
All
will go,
leaving the body behind.
The skillful person,
realizing the loss of all,
should live the holy life ardently.
Ud 5.2

All will go. What a helpful reminder. Death is not just happening to you or to the person you love. We all will experience death. Practice your faith ardently.

When you are dealing with death, a little faith can take you a long way. If you start the journey with your own beliefs around death, and what happens after death, you will be better prepared. If you have not already considered death, and what comes after death, now is the time to do so.

Chapter 10

Embracing Death Improves the Quality of Your Life

"There's a lot of death in the garden." – Joanne Meloni

My mother loved to work in the garden. She was a fan of a beautiful English garden and her garden was her pride and joy. Once while I was visiting, she looked out the window and saw some strangers wandering around the backyard. She opened the sliding glass door and asked, "Can I help you with something?"

Sheepishly, one of them replied, "We heard about your garden and we just wanted to take a peek."

There is a lot of death in the garden. Some plants are not meant to last more than one season, some become diseased and die, some die from old age. Sound familiar? Mom never let gardening deaths and disappointments get the better of her. She would not let the fact that a specific plant was going to bloom once and then die dissuade her from enjoying that plant. Instead, this was reason to enjoy the flower even more. Mom worked in the garden on the day that she died. She did not know it was her last day, but she would not have had it any other way.

To live with death is to really live. At a meditation retreat, I recall our teacher giving a Dhamma talk on impermanence. He discussed how at first so many of us find the concept of impermanence discouraging. When the meaning of impermanence is misunderstood, it can push you toward nihilism. Some develop an "if nothing lasts, why bother?" attitude. Others may take it as an excuse for a disregard of others and a call to hedonism. "Nothing lasts, I am going to die anyway, so to hell with everyone else: I am going to do whatever I feel like doing, consequences be damned."

Both of these extremes are the wrong view. The point, our teacher told us, was to go all in. Instead of avoiding experiences in life, learn the most you can from those experiences. Instead of avoiding relationships with others, be fully in those relationships, without attachment. Learn from the present moment because it will be gone. Don't think, "Why bother? This will not last." Do think, "This opportunity will not be here again. Let me really be in this moment and let it be my teacher."

It is important to remember that everyone will experience death. What rises, ceases. It is not about *if* your loved ones will die, it is *when*. The older we get, the closer we are to our death and the deaths of our family and friends.

"Those who have come to be, those who will be:
All will go, leaving the body behind.
The skillful person, realizing the loss of all, should live the holy life ardently."
Ud 5.2

To rail against death and to think that you can control the experiences that come your way is to cause yourself to suffer even more. The answer is not to avoid life's challenges; the more you wish to avoid suffering, the harder it will be. The more that you wish that the people you love will never have to leave you, the more difficult it will be for both of you when their time comes.

"If its root remains undamaged and strong, a tree, even if cut, will grow back. So too if latent craving is not rooted out, this suffering returns again and again."

— Dhp 338

The answer is to recognize the impermanence of your existence and to understand the importance of making the most of this opportunity for your growth. You are here now, and now is the time to practice non-attachment. Recognize that everything will change. We are all subject to old age, sickness and death. Old age is a gift. The more that you can become comfortable with the knowledge that you cannot keep everything and everyone you love, and that you cannot avoid the things that you do not enjoy, the closer you are to the end of suffering.

Chapter 11

Great, So How Can YOU Embrace Death?

There is a popular Buddhist story about a young girl named Kisa Gotami. She had one son who died at a very young age. Kisa Gotami was overcome with grief. Refusing to accept his death, she carried her dead son around with her. She begged others in the village for medicine that would cure him. Finally, one local follower of the Buddha told her that a great holy man would soon arrive and that he could help her. That holy man was the Buddha. When he arrived, Kisa Gotami begged him for his help. The Buddha told her that if she could bring him one mustard seed, he would cure her son. Mustard seed was very common, and she could easily find it in the household of any of her neighbors. The trick was that, the mustard had to come from a house where no family member or worker had ever died.

Kisa Gotami set off to collect mustard seeds. Every house she visited offered her more than one mustard seed. But when she advised that she could only take those seeds if they had never had an experience with death, if no family member or worker had ever died, none of them were able to give her the mustard seed. Every one of them would respond, "We have lost a child, too." Or, "My sister has already died." Or, "Our parents have died."

Finally, she understood the point of her mission. Everyone is visited by death. She also began to understand that the living are few, but the dead are many. And so she reported back to the Buddha that she understood: nobody was untouched by death.[1]

The first step toward embracing death is to realize that death is inevitable. Do not pretend that death does not exist, and do not obsess about when death will come. Just live with the fact that the living are few, and the dead are many. Buddhism offers you a complete support system to assist you as navigate old age, sickness, death and grief. Now is the time to shore up your foundation.

Consider going back to the basics. Remember the Triple Gems:

1. Take refuge in the Buddha – The Buddha showed us how to develop mindfulness, discernment and release from defilement. To take refuge in the Buddha is to take the Buddha as your role model, and to work to develop his admirable qualities in yourself.

2. Take refuge in the Dhamma – The Dhamma refers to the teachings of the Buddha. What this really comes down to is to accept the Four Noble Truths and to live your life according to the Noble Eightfold Path.

3. Take refuge in the Sangha – There are Buddhist monks and nuns who have been ordained and live the holy life and there are people who are dedicated to their practice, laypeople, who will not become monks and nuns. If you are not a monk or nun, find a reputable Buddhist group and become part of the community. You are not meant to practice on your own.

Not all Buddhists follow the same practices or have exactly the same beliefs. The Triple Gems, the Three Marks of Existence, the Four Noble Truths and the Noble Eightfold Path are consistently accepted by most traditions. We have already considered the Four Noble Truths, and we just looked at the Triple Gems. The Three Marks of Existence remind you of:

---

1   Thomas William Rhys Davids, *Buddhism: Being a Sketch of the Life and Teachings of Gautama, the Buddha* (Society for Promoting Christian Knowledge, 1903), 133–34.

1. *Anicca,* or impermanence; everything that rises, ceases

2. *Dukkha,* or there is suffering or dis-ease or stress

3. *Anatta,* or not-self, there is no need to hang on to that which causes stress; it is not yours

The above reiterate that every living thing experiences impermanence and dis-ease or stress. *Anatta* is a big topic. For now, just consider that if something is causing your suffering, why would you cling to it? Is it really yours? No. Let it go.

Do you see how this integrates with the Four Noble Truths? Watching a loved one die is like being slapped in the face by impermanence. You see them changing; you see their energy dissipating. This can lead to your own suffering, or you can work to let go of that suffering. When you adopt the Eightfold Noble Path as your approach to living your life, you are giving yourself a solid foundation. It is this foundation that will see you through your most challenging days.

The Eightfold Noble Path supports you in living your life with virtue, concentration and discernment. When you hear or read about Buddhism and the middle way, this is a reference to being able to fully adopt virtue, concentration and discernment in a balanced way. The Eightfold Noble Path consists of:

1. Right View – Understanding that there is dis-ease and stress, that it can be alleviated and how it can be alleviated.

2. Right Intention – Also called right resolve or right thinking; to seek to direct your mind away from anger and fear and toward loving-kindness and compassion and generosity.

3. Right Speech – Speaking the truth, and not speaking out of anger, and not engaging in gossip or divisive speech. Not forcing our opinion on others.

4. Right Action – To abstain from killing, lying, stealing, sexual misconduct and abuse of intoxicants. If you cannot help others, then do not harm them.

5. Right Livelihood – Earning your living in an honest and moral way, not in a way that harms yourself or others. This also includes using your income in an honest and moral way.

6. Right Effort – Working to prevent negative states of mind, overcoming negative states of mind, cultivating positive states of mind and maintaining positive states of mind.

7. Right Mindfulness –Paying moment-to-moment attention to what is. Paying attention to your body, your feelings and your mind and how they are impacted by grief or fear or self-compassion. Paying attention to the thoughts that come and go.

8. Right Concentration – Developing the ability to concentrate with a mind that is free of anger, greed and delusion.

Virtue is made up of right speech, right action and right livelihood; concentration is right effort, right mindfulness and right concentration; and discernment consists of right view and right intention.

While all of the items above may seem like a lot, there is more and there are deeper layers to all that we are discussing here. Please do not interpret this as a complete description of Buddhism. These are some of the basics, and the basics will help you build a solid foundation. Seek out a qualified and experienced teacher and find a sangha, so that you can practice with a wholesome community.

Now, let's look at how this can all tie together. Your loved one is dying or has died. You are sad. That does not make you a bad Buddhist. Accept the sadness. Recognize the suffering. Where is it coming from? You don't want your loved one to be ill and to have pain. You don't want your loved one to be dead. You miss your old life together. How can you let go of your attachment? How can you release yourself from your suffering?

Right view helps you recognize the true nature of your situation. With right intention or right thinking, perhaps you will steer yourself away from any negative thoughts toward yourself and begin to engage in some self-compassion.

Remember, self-compassion is not an excuse to indulge in harmful and unhealthy habits. It is not a reason to ignore your responsibilities and stop participating in life. It is about you learning the best way to take care of yourself as you move forward. It is about learning to love and cherish yourself, just as your loved one would have wanted you to do.

You are also going to draw upon right effort to help prevent any negative states of mind or overcome negativity that has already surfaced.

Where, in all of this, is your meditation practice? Meditation helps to cement your understanding. Right concentration is a combination of mindfulness and concentration. When both are present, you have the ability to develop powerful insight. It is this insight that allows you to really understand the true nature of things. Powerful insight is required for you to really see impermanence and suffering, and how there is nothing that is really yours. Grief is not what defines you. Being a widow is not what defines you. You do not need to hang on to any of the powerful emotions you are feeling. You can simply practice by observing them rising and ceasing.

"The function of right view is to look at events in the mind in a way that gives rise to a sense of dispassion, leading the mind to a state of non-fashioning and then on to Awakening."[2]

Learning to observe my thoughts and emotions during meditation was extremely helpful. When I could look and notice, "Oh, here comes another wave of grief," or "Oh, here comes that fear that I will never be OK again," this helped me to process. And it helped me to truly understand that I was not my sadness or fear, and these thoughts were not facts that would define my future.

One of the very first Buddhist groups that Ed and I practiced with did a very good job discussing impermanence. On more than one occasion, our teachers would remind us of the importance of including the awareness of death in our practice. You may find this beneficial, too. Think about death throughout your day. Use death as a meditation device. Consider the phrase "Today could be my last day." Death is just one of many experiences that make up a life. It is neither good nor bad; it just is.

---

2   "Wings to Awakening: Part III," accessed October 22, 2018, https://www.accesstoinsight.org/lib/authors/thanissaro/wings/part3.html#part3-h.

Developing insight into the nature of death helps you become clear about your values; it helps you to develop a sense of purpose, a mission. Death is the ultimate life coach, showing you how to live now and how to live with confidence and without fear.

With an awareness that you do not know how much time you have left, you can make better decisions and derive more value out of the time you have.

"Analysis of death is not for the sake of becoming fearful but to appreciate this precious lifetime during which you can perform many important practices. Rather than being frightened, you need to reflect that when death comes, you will lose this good opportunity for practice. In this way contemplation of death will bring more energy to your practice."[3]

Meditating on your death and that of your loved ones in preparation for facing death is amazingly helpful. When my father told me that his lung cancer was terminal, I meditated on his death—not so much on the actual moment of his death, but on the fact that he would die; I meditated on him being dead and how I would feel about it. I shed many tears, but it helped me wrap my head around the fact that he was dying. I used the same approach when Ed was dying.

One day, you might find it difficult to step away from the negativity. Occasionally, there were days where I felt sorry for myself. I could not imagine that I was every going to be happy again. On these days, Tonglen, a Tibetan Buddhist meditation practice, helped me maintain a balanced perspective. You could say that Tonglen was a meditation technique I used to practice right effort. Tonglen taught me to consider the suffering of others. In breathing in the suffering of others and breathing out a wish to alleviate their suffering, my mind was taken away from my suffering.

If you wonder what right speech, right action and right livelihood have to do with any of this, just pause and think for a moment. When you meditate, and you feel distracted or you have a difficult time concentrating, what is it that distracts you? I am not asking you about issues

---

3   Bstan- dzin-rgya-mtsho and Jeffrey Hopkins, *Mind of Clear Light: Advice on Living Well and Dying Consciously* (New York: Atria Books, 2004), 39.

with noisy neighbors and barking dogs. What are the thoughts that run through your mind? Is it that argument you had with a friend? Is it when you snapped at one of your children? All of the elements of the Eightfold Noble Path work together to position us so that we can find release from suffering.

This is not a practice guide. It is a reminder that your Buddhist practice will help prepare you for death. While there are different Buddhist perspectives about what happens during the dying process, or what happens immediately after death, there is agreement in this: the time to practice is now. You are fortunate to be in this life and to have learned the dharma.

"Make the day not-in-vain,
a little or a lot. However much the day passes,
that's how much less
is life.
Your last day approaches.
This isn't your time
to be heedless."
Thag 6.13

You see, the Buddha taught a system of interrelated practices that work together to help free us from suffering. He tried to teach it in a way that would be easily understandable to as many as possible. He knew it was not the key concepts that were difficult; it was putting them into practice that is most challenging for us. But you can do this, and you can do it now.

Chapter 12

Whose Karma Is This?

As difficult as it is, it is also an honor to be with someone during their final moments. My father, my husband and my mother: these were the people who loved me and guided me and supported me. I did not always agree with them, but I still knew that they loved me. There is no greater gift than that.

Is it odd that Dad and Ed died from the same form of lung cancer? At some point in their lives, both of them smoked. It is apparent that lung cancer was in my father's genetic makeup. His brother, Bill, died four years later, also of lung cancer. Their father also battled lung cancer. What some might call odd or an interesting twist of fate, I have learned to call karma.

Karma is a complicated topic. In its simplest form, it means action. In today's world, especially in the West, many see it as payback or retribution. We see too many bumper stickers and t-shirts that say, "Karma's a bitch." In our culture, there are not enough acknowledgments of good karma, and not enough recognition that "Instant Karma" might be a catchy song by John Lennon, but not an accurate representation of what we should expect in the real world.

Is their death about my karma or theirs? Our lives were intertwined, and so is our karma. When Mom and Ed died just five days apart, there were some who told me that I must have had some really bad karma to have lost the two people I was closest to during the same time frame. There was nothing particularly helpful about these comments. Eventually I realized that these comments were probably not meant to be judgments about me; they were meant to make others feel better about their own lives. If they could convince themselves that I must have some really bad karma, they could better come to terms with what had happened. They could seek to assure themselves that something like this would not happen to them.

Others told me that I should welcome this opportunity. That to go through something so painful was, in fact, a tremendous gift. This would surely lead to my own spiritual advancement.

Was I bad person in a past life? Was I bad person earlier in this life? These are unanswerable questions. There is nothing I can do about my past. All I can do is work to be the best person that I can be now. The karma that I experience is a blend of my past and current actions.

I cannot go back in time and change anything about my current or past lives. Time travel story lines, while fun, are inherently flawed. You are only supposed to change one thing, but if you change other things, the universe is damned forever. You are never supposed to meet yourself in another dimension, or the universe is damned forever. Forget about all that. It is much easier to just work on your life as you live it right now.

Not knowing what will come, but knowing that whatever happens is part of your karma, is less stressful than worrying about what is coming. Grief is something to learn from and not simply to be endured. It is not a series of mile markers on a race- track. There is no need to rush through any part of your life; it is all as it is meant to be. You need to keep practicing.

The *Acintita Sutta* (AN 4.77) says:

> "There are these four unconjecturables that are not to be conjectured about, that would bring madness and vexation to anyone who conjectured about them. Which four?"

The sutta goes on to state that the precise working out of the results of karma is one of the things not to be conjectured about.

It never occurred to me to go to one of my spiritual teachers and ask why this had happened. To practice Buddhism is to accept impermanence and to know that your karma cannot be fully mapped out, nor predicted. To fully embrace impermanence is to understand that everything that arises ceases. EVERYTHING also means EVERYONE. We are all going to die, and we are all going to lose people we love. That's how it works.

Chapter 13

Learning to Face Death with Equanimity

Knock Knock
(A Haiku)

Oh, it's you again.
Really? No place else to be?
OK, death—come in.

A year and a quarter after Mom and Ed died, my Uncle Bill died. Then a former co-worker died, and a friend died, and I lost track of some of the deaths. It is not that I became desensitized; it is that I grew differently sensitized. I became aware of the rhythm of life with death happening around me and aware of death as another facet of life. Once born, we will die. It doesn't work any other way.

"Impermanent are all component things, They arise and cease, that is their nature: They come into being and pass away, Release from them is bliss supreme." — Mahaa-Parinibbaana Sutta (DN 16)

It makes no sense for you to be angry at death or about death. In fact, one Buddhist perspective is that you should welcome death and be upset at birth. Birth means that instead of achieving Nirvana, you have returned to the world yet again. You are here to experience more *dukkha,* or discomfort.

In *Buddhism and Death*, Walshe says:

> We all fear death, but actually, we should also fear the rebirth that follows. In practice, this does not always happen. Fear of rebirth is less strong than death. This is part of our usual short-sighted view for those who do actually believe in rebirth, and the fact must be faced. Full Enlightenment will only be achieved when there is the will to transcend all forms of "rebirth" — even the pleasantest. Though as a first step then, acceptance of the fact of rebirth may help to overcome the fear of death, the attachment to rebirth itself must then also be gradually overcome.[4]

I know now that I am guilty of using rebirth as a way of becoming less afraid of losing the ones I love. Thinking that with rebirth, there was no real goodbye, I grew less anxious about saying goodbye to friends who were moving away. The belief that I will be with others again in another life helped me accept the fact of their death. This is the wrong view.

While it is true that once there is birth, death will follow, it does not have to be that once there is death, rebirth will follow. To become comfortable with death and to be less attached to life is to advance on the path away from suffering. You should not be looking at rebirth to bring you comfort; you should wish that those who you love escape the endless samsara of birth, death and rebirth. Use this lifetime to move forward with your practice.

I won't tell you that now death is easy for me. That death is no big deal, that I am not sad when someone dies, or that I do not cry. I won't tell you that because it is not true. What I will say is that my relationship with death has become much more balanced. I see that death has its place in the overall landscape of my life.

Death is something that I have come to accept. It is one of the many events that make up our lives. In one moment, I might be with a friend who has just lost her husband and in the next moment, I receive a text that my other friend is newly engaged. On the same day, I might learn

4   "Buddhism and Death," accessed October 22, 2018, https://accesstoin-sight.org/lib/authors/walshe/wheel261.html.

that a former co-worker has died and then I receive a text about some-one else's new baby.

All of these moments are important and are meant to be experienced with equanimity. This does not mean without feeling. It means to direct your energy and emotions in the best possible way. Be happy for your newly engaged friend. Don't be manic about it. Be sad at the loss of your co-worker. Understand the truth, that you cannot feel every-thing for everybody. You cannot prevent others from having difficul-ties, and you are rarely the cause for their gains. YOU are not karma.

I remember during his final days driving to pick up a refill of Dad's morphine prescription. All around me in the drug store were people just going about their business. Teenage girls looking at the makeup selection, a woman buying greeting cards and a father buying his little children ice cream. I recall thinking, Dad used to buy me ice cream, too. And now he never will again. It was hard to understand, how all of these people could just be going about their business.

When Mom and Ed died, I recall having a similar reaction. I would see people running their errands, buying groceries, filling up their gas tanks. Didn't they know that I was utterly torn up? But eventually, I began to see the routines of others as reassuring. Watching people navigate the everyday business of life gave me hope. There were oth-ers who were well and happy. And I would be, too. It was good to be surrounded by people who did not seem to be impacted by death. Of course, I had no idea how many of them were watching the rest of us and thinking, "How can they just be going about their business, don't they know my loved one has died?"

There were days when sorting the mail would bring me to tears. It was like I lived with a house of ghosts. Mail would come for my mother-in-law who died in 2010, my father (2012), my mom and Ed (2014). In fact, some days, none of the mail was addressed to me.

Eventually, there were fewer days when I cried while looking at the mail and, finally, it made me laugh. When my mother-in-law received an invitation to take a trip to the Turks and Caicos, I had to giggle.

If she were still alive, she would have wanted to go on that trip. If she were still alive, she would have been 105.

Equanimity helped me accept the importance of living the life that I had been given and to realize that already having experienced difficulties was no guarantee that there would not be more difficulties.

Going on a meditation retreat with two friends, I looked forward to experiencing peace and bliss. Instead, one of them became ill and left the first day, and the other had nightmares and tantrums and a miserable time. My first thought was one of profound annoyance. Didn't I deserve a calm and soothing retreat? Why should I have to spend my time helping my friend feel better? When we returned home, another friend was waiting to tell me that he was a drug addict and that he had hit bottom. Could I please help him?

And I thought, "Seriously, life, I am just barely getting my strength back? Can you give me a break?"

My friends would say things like, "Well, you are done now. You have already had some difficult experiences. There is no way that life (or God, if that was their belief system), would send you anything else to deal with. That just would not be fair."

But it is not about fair or about what you have had to deal with. There are many people who have dealt with situations that are much more difficult. People have lost their entire families in one tragic moment.

Your karma will send you what it sends you. That does not mean that your life is fatalistically predetermined. It means that based on your past and current actions, your karma will take root. And you will live the fruits of your karma. Equanimity brings you a balanced perspective. It helps you to set your priorities. You understand that it makes no sense to spend your energy on your past actions. Own these actions and the karma that stems from them. Do your best with what comes your way. Do not use your energy wishing that your loved ones would not die. Use your actions skillfully, to help yourself and to help others.

Expectations of a life completely without *dukkha* are unreasonable. It was my *views* that made a situation either easy or difficult, to be avoided or to be embraced. Equanimity and compassion and loving-kindness helped me to see my role in my own suffering.

When my aunt told me not to worry, that she would be here for twenty more years, my intuition and my understanding of impermanence told me otherwise. I knew that when it was her time, it would be difficult and I would miss her—and I could handle it. I had developed an acceptance of death; now we were old friends. He would come when he would come. It was nothing personal.

PART IV

THIS IS ABOUT YOU

Chapter 14

Take Care of Yourself

This is the one time in your life when it can be about you. If you are that person who rarely takes center stage, if you are the one who usually takes care of others and defers to their needs, this is the time to take care of yourself. And it may not come naturally to you.

Some people around you are going to make this about them. You will have your difficult people, you will have your people who are usually not difficult but become so now, and you will have your helpful people who want to take care of you. And there you are, right smack in the middle of all of it.

Feel free to minimize the amount of time you spend with people who drain your energy. This is a great rule for us to follow at all times, but now it is even more important. You are running on empty both physically and emotionally, and you need take care of yourself first. Remember put your own oxygen mask on first!

Trust your intuition. A friend who I had fallen out of touch with learned that I was navigating the death of my mother and my husband. The good news for me is that she had forgotten my address. I say that because she began bombarding me with messages about how she need-ed to come be with me, and I needed someone to come take care of me, and I could not be by myself. In the past, I had watched her method of taking care of others, and while she meant well and had a heart of gold, she was loud and she was overbearing. Her way to take care of someone was to take over every aspect of their life. As an introvert, all I wanted was quiet. I could not imagine having someone in the house with me, telling me what was best for me.

You would think that during a time such as this, your inner critic would just be quiet. But that's not what inner critics do, is it? Your inner critic might be telling you things like:

- "You should stop crying so much."
- "Why aren't you crying more? What's wrong with you?"
- "You should be able to concentrate on your work."
- "You should be more productive."
- "You should, you should, you should…"

There is no such thing as *should*, there is only what is. Pay close attention to what you are feeling.

Consider this: how would you treat a friend who just lost someone she loved? Would you be harsh? Would you tell her to stop crying and get back to work? Probably not. Be your own best friend. This means that you do not use your own self-talk to say things that you would not say to others.

Being self-compassionate is not a free pass to being self-destructive. It does not mean that it is OK to eat a pint of ice cream every day or to drink a pint of vodka every day. Keep an eye out for self-destructive behaviors.

You still have responsibilities, and you will handle those responsibilities. This is the time to really sort through the difference between what are nice things to do and what are required things for you to do. Paying your rent or your mortgage, let's call that required. Going to an event because someone said it would be good for you, let's call that optional.

Being self-compassionate includes being self-aware and empathetic. For example, during the first two months after Mom and Ed died, I would reach a certain point in my day where I was just done, mentally and physically done for the day. The problem was that, initially, this was at about 4 p.m. At 4 p.m., I felt like I could not do one more thing. I also knew that it was far too early to go to bed. When I felt like

I could not do one more thing, I would pick just one more thing to do and then, after I completed it, I allowed myself to be done for the day. Next, I would meditate. At first, I could only meditate for a few minutes, and it was a major sob fest.

I did not go to sleep, but I did allow myself to drift through the rest of the afternoon and evening in an unstructured manner. If I felt like reading, then I read. If I felt like watching old episodes of *Ally McBeal* or *Friends* or *Fraser* on Netflix, then that is what I did.

Keep an eye on yourself. You are going to have days where all you want to do is stay under the covers. This is normal. Allow yourself a day to mope. However, do not allow yourself to spend seven days a week under the covers. Most days you want to get out of bed at a normal time and get dressed. Groom yourself, whether you are leaving the house or not. Eat healthy meals. Resume your exercise routine. Keep in touch with the right people, the people who do not drain your energy. If you are having severe difficulties getting up and getting dressed and handling day-to-day living, then get help. Seek out grief support groups and counseling. Ask trusted friends for help. Nobody said you had to go through this alone.

Being self-compassionate does not mean you never do anything difficult. The day comes when you need to go back to work, or interact with the public, or attend social functions. Be aware of your limitations.

Because I did so much work from home, and because Mom and Ed died during the holiday season, my work demands were fairly light. I was able to keep up with just about everything. I had one class I was teaching in person. I had two classes I was taking.

I found that I was able to return to instructing and also to attending classes within a week. On my way to teaching, I would cry in the car all the way to class. When I was in front of the class, I was able to concentrate on them and, for that short period of time, I was able to forget about my sadness. Once I left the classroom and got back in my car, I would cry all the way home. I learned to keep a good supply of tissues and eye makeup with me at all times. And I learned not to judge myself for needing to cry.

About two months after, I was scheduled to travel to teach a corporate class across the country. I went, because I thought it might be good for me to leave the house and because I believed that I could be sad anywhere. I was right; in some ways it was good for me, and it was true, I could be sad anywhere. Living my life was not about denying the grief, it was about supporting myself in a way that I could get back to the business of living, and, for me, the business of living included making room for grieving.

Chapter 15

The Business of Death

There is this odd space that occurs between the business of death and the reshaping of your life. After Mom and Ed died, I began to think of myself as the project manager of death. I had been a project manager, and I had my own training and development organization teaching others to be project managers. This enabled me to organize all of the paperwork that comes with death and to understand the order in which things needed to occur to hit any required due dates.

The business of death can be time-consuming. There are notifications to make, papers to be signed, banks and insurance and other agencies to contact. There are things to sort through.

For example, during the first three months after Mom and Ed died, I had forms to fill out, phone calls to make, death-related errands to run. I decided that I would take care of all death-related business in the morning. And then in the afternoon, I would get back to my work. I knew that I needed some routine to keep me focused. I knew that, for me, the best thing to do was to take care of the hard stuff first. I also began to realize that once I hit a specific time in the day, I would feel mentally and physically exhausted. I would push myself to do one more thing, and then I would allow myself some unstructured time. This is when I would let myself to do whatever I felt like doing. I did require myself to stay awake until at least 9 p.m.

Some days you will have energy highs: you want to get as much accomplished as possible. Other days, you will have energy lows, and it will be all you can do to get yourself dressed. Being self-compassionate means being aware of these waves and learning how to surf them. Take advantage of those high-energy moments and understand that they will end. Be less demanding and judgmental of yourself during your low-energy moments. Those moments will end, too.

You can work with your energy fluctuations by keeping a prioritized list of your tasks. Develop an understanding of the types of energy these tasks will take. In this way, you can continue to move at a pace that works for you and helps you to handle your responsibilities.

When you are faced with a situation that feels overwhelming even on a high-energy day, get help. I have a friend who has done such an amazing job with this. Her husband died unexpectedly, between Christmas and New Year's Eve. In a short period, she was faced with planning his funeral, handling issues with difficult family members and learning the truth about her finances. Very quickly, she developed an understanding of what she wanted to manage on her own and what she wanted her friends to assist her with. She also knew which friend she needed or trusted to help her with specific tasks. When I went to spend a day with her, she knew what she wanted to accomplish that day, and she had planned it based on how she felt I could be the most helpful and supportive.

Death is a business. One of the transactions I dreaded the most was dealing with the mortuary. I had two to deal with. My parents had both prearranged their cremations. For Mom, I knew who to call and what was supposed to happen. After seeing how they handled my father's arrangements, I knew that they would be ethical and responsive.

Ed and I had discussed what he wanted, but it had not been prearranged. I knew of a local mortuary who seemed to have a good reputation, and that is who I called the night that Ed died. The next day, I anticipated quite a battle. All we had wanted was a simple cremation and for his ashes to be scattered at sea. No service. I knew that the representative I worked with was going to try to upsell me at every turn. I was prepared for questions about pre-cremation viewings and upgraded urns and all kinds of extras. To my utter surprise, the man I met with was kind and respectful. He listened to what I had to say. He repeated it back to me. He explained the process to me, and he told me how much it would cost. That was it. No trying to make me feel guilty for our choices, no trying to sell me additional services. I left feeling so much relief and gratitude. I had already seen how some mortuaries play on the emotions of family members.

Something I did not know was that many companies have resources whose job it is to help you with the business of death. One of the nicest names for this that I came across was survivor support. In most cases, when I called a customer service representative and told him or her that I was calling on behalf of a deceased loved one, I would be transferred to the survivor support team. Most of these phone calls were about closing or transferring accounts. Money was involved. I expected that most of the people I worked with in this capacity would be focused on the best way to get money out of me. For the most part, I found this be untrue. I found that most of the people who worked in this capacity were very kind. They were helpful and patient and walked me through the required processes and paperwork. When there was a balance due, they did not act like a collection agency. Some of them even sounded sincere as they expressed condolences and concern.

In many ways, it is good that death comes with some administrative work. Performing mundane paperwork is a good distraction. Most of it is not so complicated that you are not up to the task; most of it takes enough of your attention so that you can have periods of time where your days have structure and purpose. Hopefully as the paperwork begins to wrap up, you are beginning to be able to direct your attention to other aspects of your life, but you may struggle, wanting to return to your old routines.

Take the Time YOU Need to Get Your Strength Back

There is no exact schedule or timetable to follow to reach a point in your life where you feel 100% like your old self. You will never feel like your old self because you have changed. You will be a person who has lost a person or people whom you love, and who has lived to tell the tale. However, the day will come when you do feel comfortable in your skin, and you will live a new life.

For me, there was a day when I realized that I felt like I consistently had my strength back. I realized that, for some time, I had been feeling healthy and grounded. I felt less hesitant about the direction of my life and I no longer felt like I was going through the motions. I was no longer treading water and trying to get by; I was taking charge and making plans and looking forward to the future.

I reached this point about one and a half years after Mom and Ed died. I share this with you not as a goal to meet or to exceed, but in the interest of honesty. It takes what it takes. Your journey will be your own.

One day, I was reading a book on launching business ideas. The beginning of the book recommended taking a self-inventory. True to good coaching practices, I was asked to consider what I wanted. Where did I see myself in one year, in five years? This simple exercise was like a punch to the throat, and I physically fell to the ground. I realized that I was not living my life with plans for one year or five years or even one month. I was not living. I was subsisting. I had no plans or goals. At that moment, I realized that I needed to take control of my life.

Just before he died, Ed and I had reached a place that we had been happily anticipating: a time when he was semi-retired and most of my work took place online. We had the freedom to plan our days in a way that suited us. We could travel whenever we wished.

After he died, I was left with this freedom and I was uncertain what to do with it. I also realized that over the past few years, this freedom had been consumed by seeing others through their final days. Now, I had lots of time and no one to take care of but myself. It was overwhelming.

Some days it felt like I would never have a regular life again. Truthfully, I did not know what that even meant. Initially, I thought it meant never feeling sad, never missing the people who I had loved and lost. Now I can tell you that normal does not mean never feeling sad and never missing the ones you loved. It means accepting the way things are and living your life as fully as possible. It involves creating a life that helps you live with purpose, creating a life that allows you to prioritize what is important to you and then to live accordingly. For me, this means spending time with friends and loved ones, continuing my spiritual practice, working and traveling. You will define what normal means for you.

I did not come to this place overnight. It was a gradual process. I had times when I thought I was there. I was at full strength. But then something would happen, like the death of another loved one, and I would experience a setback.

But each time that I faced a challenge, I began to feel more resilient, and I recovered more quickly. You will, too.

Getting your strength back and being compassionate to yourself go hand in hand. It makes no sense to beat yourself up over feeling weak or over having difficulty coping. But you will not get your strength back until you do the required work.

Think of it as your own mental and emotional fitness program. You have to exercise on a regular basis to reach a certain level of fitness, and the workouts are not always easy. You might feel like others around you are making better progress than you are making. Don't worry about them; keep focused on your own experience. We all have different levels of strength. Take charge of your program to regain your strength.

If I were to try to define how I regained my strength, I would say that this was the formula:

Time + Self-compassion + Self-awareness + Acceptance + Action + Spiritual Path

Time, because, as annoying as it is, it is also true that time can heal all wounds. How much time? That is different for each of us. Know that there are aspects of your healing that cannot be rushed.

Self-compassion, because this is not the time to beat yourself up. Remember to treat yourself as you would treat your best friend. Be your own best friend. Do not shirk your responsibilities or engage in harmful behavior. Treat yourself in ways that will help you to overcome your suffering.

Self-awareness, because you need to understand your limitations and boundaries, and then know when to push yourself to exceed those limitations. Some people learn to ride a bicycle by using training wheels; some people jump on the bike and start peddling.

Acceptance, because you cannot move on until you accept that your life has changed. Your loved ones have died. You are still alive. Death is an integral part of life. You and death will meet again.

Action, because you need to do something. You do not just sit on your meditation cushion; you do not just intellectualize or internalize. You need to act. You involve other people, and you go back to work, and you go back to the gym, and you socialize and travel and volunteer. You actively create your new life.

Spiritual path, because you need meaning and a way to process your grief. In my specific case, Buddhism, the Four Noble Truths and the Noble Eightfold Path helped me recognize and reflect on my pain.

You may have noticed I have listed the elements of the formula, but not the proportions or ratios for those elements. I cannot give you exact amounts. I can tell you that it is different for each of us. And it is different for each segment of your journey.

Early on, you may have more self-compassion and less action. That is OK; you do not know what to do—yet. Next, you find yourself working with more acceptance. All of this transpires during the passing of time.

Know that it is normal to experience some setbacks and fluctuations. Keep at it. One day, you will feel it: there it is, your strength.

Chapter 16

On Role Playing

"Just because you are my rock, does not mean you cannot cry. Even rocks crack." These were the words Ed would say to me as we progressed through his cancer. For him, I was happy to remain strong. He knew me well enough to understand my thought process: "I will have plenty of time on my own to deal with the sadness." He knew that I was sad, and I did let him know how much I would miss him. Together we agreed to make the most of our remaining time.

If you have accepted a role for yourself in your relationships with others, be aware that people may have a difficult time seeing you in a different light.

This rock had plenty of cracks. But since they were not surface cracks, people thought I was OK. As if losing the two people that I was closest to was a breeze. As if it did not impact me at all. They did not see me crying on the way to and from events.

When you take on roles in life, many of the people around you will want you to stay in that role. If your role is to be the strong one, and people are used to you taking care of them, or at least not needing help from them, that is where they expect you to stay. They, too, will most likely remain within the confines of their roles. This can translate into confusion and hurt feelings for all of you.

Within two weeks after Mom and Ed's death, I resumed going to class. My thought process was that:

1. It was what they would have wanted me to do
2. I could be sad anywhere

I did this knowing that, for the most part, I would be able to keep it together when I was in a group of people. Unfortunately, my decision only reinforced my attachment to being the strong one, and it convinced some people that I did not need their help. This resulted in some people ignoring me and pretending that nothing had changed. This hurt my feelings. I could not understand why some of the people who I thought were closest to me did not reach out to me. Why didn't some of them check on me to see if I was OK? Why wouldn't someone who was a close friend be willing to change her schedule to spend time with me?

We all continued in our roles. My self-centered, high-maintenance friend somehow managed to make this about her. She called me and advised me that she was going to come and sit with me. She did not want me to be alone. Then she called back twenty minutes later to let me know that she had to check with another friend because there was somewhere else crucial that she had to be. Then she called back about twenty minutes after that and said she would see me on Wednesday. Then she called back and said, "I can't make it. It's Thanksgiving week, you know." Yes, it was Thanksgiving, and I became thankful that she did not call again for several days, as I did not have the energy for one more conversation about her and her schedule.

My friend who played the role of the energy vampire very nearly did suck the life out of me. One day after class, she followed me to my car and proceeded to tell me the story of what happened when her father died. At first I thought, "Well maybe there is some kernel of wisdom in this for me? There must be some message of hope or something helpful, and that is why she has decided to tell me this story."

No! There was merely her need to unburden herself on me. This was the time she had selected to tell me the minute-by-minute accounting of the last two days of her father's life. I did not have the mental or physical energy for it, but she could not see that I was not up for this. At some point, another friend, who often played the role of facilitator, had come over and was listening. This friend tried to interject comments such as, "Margaret looks tired. Maybe you can finish this another time." But she was not going to stop, and I was beginning to break.

When I was finally able to drive away, it was to meet a friend for dinner. He took one look at me and said, "Today is the first day that I can honestly say to you, you look like you have been through hell."

A few weeks later, my energy vampire and another friend asked me out to lunch. Again, our time together was spent listening to the tale of the death of another of her family members. It was still too soon.

Toward the end of lunch, the other friend looked at her and asked, "Why are you doing this now?" Her response? "Because I was not even able to function for three months. After my father died, I quit my job. I did not work for almost a year, and she can hold it together. I don't understand why."

If only I had been more open about my lack of strength. But there I was clinging to my role and, in turn, my friends stuck to their roles. Perhaps if I had done a better job letting people know I was hurting, some of them would have seen the cracks in this rock. At least one person did say to me, "Well, I knew you were a big girl, and you could deal with it. Plus, if you needed something you should have let me know."

When people asked me if needed help, I did not know what to say. What I wanted to say was, "Can you make the people I love not be dead?" The truth was, I had no idea what I needed. I also wanted to protect them. I was so used to being able to see myself through difficult situations; I just assumed that I would see myself through this one, too.

Several months after Ed died, I had the front yard re-landscaped. This involved taking out a large bougainvillea which used to cover most of the front window. When the bougainvillea came out, the window was exposed. It was dirty. About two days after the bougainvillea was removed, one of my neighbors was walking by. I happened to be in the front yard. She stopped and asked if I liked my nice clean window. I thought she was being sarcastic. Then I realized that she was not; someone had, in fact, cleaned my front window. She proceeded to tell me that her husband had come over and cleaned the window for me.

This may have been a well-intentioned act. But I felt insulted and ashamed and violated. Apparently, my dirty window bothered him, so he jumped right on it.

After years of hiding behind the bougainvillea, the window frame needed repainting and another wall that had been covered by other foliage also needed paint. I felt so anxious and stressed over this "favor" that I immediately dropped everything I was doing and went to Home Depot to purchase the supplies I needed to take care of the window frame and the wall. I did not want anyone thinking that I was not capable of taking care of my property. I did not want people just coming into my yard to fix or clean things that thought needed cleaning or fixing. I was not incompetent, I was sad; didn't people know the difference?

I cannot blame others for my attachment to my role of being the strong one. This is what is known as a fetter. A fetter is a chain or a bond that ties you to suffering. And developing a strong sense of I, and me, and mine is a terrific way to suffer.

If, during this time, you cling to your role as the strong one, or the emotional one, or the drama queen, or the energy vampire, you are binding yourself to suffering with a fetter. Remember, there is suffering, and we suffer because of attachment to things, and ideas, and pets, and people.

The more that you hang on to your role, the more you think, "I am strong, I should be able to handle this," or "I should be recovering faster," or "I should not feel sad anymore." All of these thoughts are just adding to your suffering.

When you let go of all expectations of yourself as the strong one, or any other role, and just let yourself experience your grief, you will find your real inner strength.

PART V

PEOPLE MEAN WELL

Chapter 17

People Have Opinions (About How You Should Live Your Life)

People are going to want to give you advice, and that advice comes from their opinions on how you should live and act now that your loved one has died. Not only is what you are reading right now advice about advice, in a way, you could say that this entire book is my way of giving you advice, too. My advice, like all advice, comes from the opinions I developed as I went through my own experience. Is my advice any better than what you will receive from others? Only you can decide.

Consider the intent of the person who is sharing their perspective with you. Most people mean well. That does not make their advice appropriate or relevant or helpful. The truth is, people offer up all kinds of useless advice. As part of my experience, I have observed that the advice people gave me was typically based on one of these perspectives:

They want you to follow a specific tradition or pattern of behavior

Most of the advice that I received that fell into this category was about other people's beliefs about how I should look, act and talk as a widow. It varied from how long I should keep wearing my wedding ring, to wearing only dark colors, and whether or not I could bring a plus-one with me to social events. These were beliefs that came from religious or cultural protocols.

After Ed died, I returned to a local Buddhist temple. I was not surprised that some of the monks treated me differently. This temple was associated with a specific Buddhist tradition with ties in Cambodia. Most of those who attended had not been born in the United States. In their culture, the role of the widow was well-defined. A widow is a second-class citizen. I stopped returning to the temple after one of the monks began to yell at me for appearing in public without my husband. I respect their culture, but was not willing to apply it to my own life.

Some of my acquaintances came from a cultural belief that stated you stay away from someone who has had a family member die. The quarantine period is six months. I know of one couple who waited almost six months to the day before they made contact with me. In fact, I knew who some of my true friends were because they came from this tradition, but they came to my side well before the six-month period was over.

Other examples of this type of advice include gems like, "Don't go to social functions for several months, because your presence will make people uncomfortable." According to the person who shared this tidbit with me, people would invite me to things so that I knew they were thinking about me, but they did not want me to show up. Um, OK?

They have preconceived notions about how you should act

People will make assumptions about how they think your life should be. This is similar to the kind of guidance that comes from people who want you to follow a specific tradition, but it is less tied to cultural or religious affiliation. I was surprised at some of the "guidelines" that were expressed to me by people who I thought had no specific religious or cultural tradition.

I had a business trip that had been scheduled before Ed's death. As things played out, the trip was to occur two months after he died. I was shocked when a relative made this comment to me:

"Of course you are not going. What are you doing, considering a business trip, when you should be at home grieving?"

As if it was her place to judge how and when I would grieve. I already knew that I could be sad in any location. I thought that while the trip would push me regarding my emotional strength, in some ways, it would be good for me. And I did need to keep working. It was a difficult trip, but it was also good for me. It helped me to reclaim some of my strength and to validate that I could keep going.

Another popular thought was around where I should live or who I should live with. This surfaced in a couple of different ways. The friend who asked, "Would you like me to help you find a roommate?" or the colleague who asked, "So who do you have staying with you?" are a few examples.

It showed up in a not-so-subtle way from the local realtors who came to the door or left flyers about helping me to sell my home during this difficult time. And it showed up when I encountered a former neighbor, who I had not seen for over a year.

"So, where are you living now?" she asked.

"In the same house I have lived in since you have known me," I replied.

At that, while avoiding eye contact, she stuttered and stammered out, "Oh, good for you."

Sometimes the advice I received was more in the form of someone questioning my behavior. In fact, YOU might find that you have ideas about what you should or should not be doing. You might find yourself wondering what you think is appropriate behavior.

About seven months after Ed died, I had the opportunity to travel internationally with some friends and classmates. At first, I fell prey to my own notions about what was acceptable. When my classmate turned to me and asked me to go with her, initially I thought, "I can't do that." But then, very quickly, another inner voice replied with, "Of course you can. You have the time available, and you have the budget."

When I told others about the trip, there were one or two people who said, "Are you sure you should be doing that?" Fortunately, I was able to confidently reply, "Yes, I am."

It was around this time that I began to use "I am not the one who died," as my mantra.

They are afraid for you

Some of the advice that you receive will be fear-based. The people who care for you do not want to see you go through even more suffering. If they have gone through a similar situation, they do not want you to have the same difficulties that they encountered. That's where I stand in writing this book for you and hoping that in some way it will help you experience less suffering. Or they know of someone else who had a painful experience, and they are afraid you will have that same experience. Or they are grappling with their own fears.

Right after Ed died, a close friend kept urging me to take off. To take a trip and relax and have some fun. While it was clear to me that this was not the right time for a vacation, and that being away from home during these first few weeks would be harmful to me, it was also clear that in some way he was trying to protect me from being sad. He honestly thought that a vacation would be a diversion that would help cheer me up.

Some of my friends come from a culture where a woman needs to have a man. Without a man, she has no power. An unattached woman of a certain age is not considered valuable. I did not truly understand how prevalent this attitude still was until three separate female friends gave me the same talk, which goes like this:

"Don't wait too long to start dating again. You are not getting any younger. You are pretty now, but soon your looks will fade, and men will not look at you. And don't be too picky. You are going to have a hard time because you are too smart. And don't let them know that you can take care of yourself."

Wow. The first time I received that little lecture, I froze. I just sat there waiting for my friend to wear herself out so that I could change the topic.

Some of my male friends gave me a talk that was just the opposite:

"Forget about dating. You are done. There are no good men out there for you. At this point in life, all that is left are the losers and the unstable ones. You would never be able to put up with them."

Two pieces of opposing advice: hurry up and date versus you should never date or try to be with a man again. Both recommendations are based in the fear that I would be a woman without a man. Oh, the horror! Or that I would only have horrible men to date.

They want you to do things their way

Ed and I made a very untraditional choice. And that was that there would be no funeral or memorial service for him. It was something that he felt strongly about, and not only did I want to carry out his wishes, I also agreed with him. This bothered some people. It was not the choice they would have made. One or two of his friends pulled me aside and said, "After he is gone, you are going to have a service, aren't you? That's what I would do."

No, I was not going to hold a service. We agreed to no service, and that was how it was going to be.

After Ed died, a family member sent me a text asking for the day and time of the service. When I replied that there was no service, he responded, "I am not sure that I agree with that." To which I texted, "It's not your place to agree or disagree." To his credit, he did back down.

The opinions that people expressed about whether or not there would be a service for Ed could have been rooted in religious beliefs and cultural norms. But it also demonstrates that people want you to do things a certain way, and that way is their way.

They want something from you

Closely aligned with the advice that comes from people who want you to do things their way is the advice that comes from people who want something from you. They see opportunity in your misfortune. By that, I mean an opportunity for them.

In fact, as I am writing this, one of my friends is experiencing this right now. She has a friend who checks in with her on a regular basis to ask her what she is going to do with all of her things. As if the fact that her husband has died means that she no longer needs her dishes or her furniture or her television. Her friend advises her to downsize and get rid of some of her possessions. This same friend then not-so-subtly asks her to give her things like dishes or furniture.

Another of her friends asked her why she wanted to keep living in her house all by herself. Wasn't she afraid? Was she safe living by herself? Maybe she should not live by herself. And then an amazing coincidence occurred. That same friend knew of someone who needs a place to stay. Funny how that worked out.

When I was selling my mother's house, a potential buyer came with an offer that was good, but not great. I instructed my realtor to counter-offer. The buyer came back, but again with something that was good, but not great. I did not like it. I did some soul searching to make sure that I was not being resistant to selling the house, and that I was not unrealistic. I knew the comparables for other properties in the area, so I knew that I was not expecting too much. I also knew that my brother was waiting for the house to sell and for the estate to close, so I knew that I was not being resistant or dragging my feet. I sat with it, and I arrived at a price that I felt would be fair to all parties.

I called my realtor and gave him my answer to the counteroffer. He was not happy. It became apparent that he wanted me to take the offer. He was ready to be done with this. I was a bit surprised by his attitude because he was not taking a discount on his commission. In his desire to move things along, he said to me, "You know, why don't you take this offer and move on. The sooner that you do, the sooner that you can let go and put this sad chapter in your life behind you."

His words to me only made me dig my heels in. My reply was, "Well, I can always take the house off the market and rent it for an indefinite period." He could not back down quickly enough. He took my counteroffer to the buyer, and she accepted it.

They genuinely want you to be well and happy

About two months after Ed died, one of his friends, who had also been a co-worker, came to see me. He brought me some of the contents of Ed's desk and workspace. He took me to lunch, and we caught up. We had been to lunch a time or two when he said to me, "I have a dining club. We get together and try out new restaurants, you should come with us."

My immediate response was, "Oh, I don't want to do that. I do not want to have to meet people and tell them what happened."

His reply was something along the lines of, "Don't be stupid. Nobody is going to ask you a bunch of questions. I am going to put you on the list, and one day when you are ready, you should join us."

I could not see it at the time, but he was right. And after a few months, I did realize that I needed to come out and socialize and make new friends. In fact, getting together with a group like this one was one of the best ways to accomplish this.

His advice was aimed at helping me. There was no agenda. There was no expression of what I should be doing. There was merely an invitation.

There is one piece of classic advice that turned out to be helpful to me. That is the council that during the first year, do not make big decisions. There is a caveat to this. Do not postpone decisions that you must make to take of yourself and your ability to be well. Do not delay your healthcare. Do not ignore debt. If it is true that you cannot afford to continue living in your current location, then do something.

If I had not followed this advice, I might have sold my home and moved, for no logical reason other than the people around me expected me to do so and for a brief period I fell prey to my thoughts around what it meant to be a widow. About three months after Ed died, I had some self-talk like this going on: "Well, I am a widow. Widows are old. Old people downsize. I guess I should sell my house and move to something more appropriate."

What a bunch of crap that was. Fortunately, one day I came out the other side and realized: "This is my home. I am happy here, and I am comfortable here. I am not walking through the house seeing Ed in every corner. But to make sure that I do not live in a museum dedicated to us, I should make some simple changes." And that is what I did. I repainted the interior in colors that I liked. I replaced the windows because I thought that was important; I re-landscaped the front yard using drought-tolerant plants because that was what I wanted. Someday, I might move. Right now, this is my home.

Listen to the advice and the opinions that people offer. Do not feel like you have to take their advice and do not feel like you owe anyone explanations for your decisions. If you have a friend who can be a trusted confidant, that is terrific. Know that he or she still comes with some form of bias; we all do.

Before you make a decision, no matter whose advice you are following, consider:

- Am I making this decision out of fear?
- Am I making this decision based on someone else's expectations?
- Am I making this decision based on a system of beliefs that I do not embrace?
- How will this decision help me live the life I want to live?

Chapter 18

Some People Will Disappoint You

Most people mean well. There are some damaged people out there. Some people harbor ill will toward others. But most people mean well. When you are going through a difficult time, the people who genuinely care about you are not sitting around thinking about how they can mess with you. Or are they?

You might find that this is a time when you question the intentions of some of the people around you. With that thought in mind, thank you for letting me share some of my experiences with you.

"You have to read this book. You have to read this book NOW! I can give it to you this morning. Drive down here and pick it up." My colleague was barking at me over the phone. I had just explained to her that I needed to postpone a meeting with her for an unspecified amount of time. Why an undetermined amount of time? Ed had just officially entered into home hospice mode. Now was not the time to take a ninety-minute round-trip drive to pick up a book on how to say goodbye. I was already living it. Plus, I already had the book. That same colleague gave it to me when Dad died.

It took me about fifteen minutes to get her to back off about the book. As part of that fifteen minutes, I had to explain to her what it meant for Ed and me to be participating in home hospice. Every hospice situation is different. As his primary caretaker, our case did not allow me ninety minutes to go pick up a book on death and dying.

Even after my explanation, she was reluctant to let it go. I always wondered why, if she thought this book was going to make such an extraordinary difference, she didn't ship it to me. Or why didn't she make the drive to drop it off? If it was so important, why did it need to involve me making the commute to pick it up?

Then there was the friend who came from a different Buddhist tradition. Her practice was that when someone dies, you are supposed to leave the body undisturbed for two days. This was not something that Ed and I embraced. Since he died at home, the standard procedure is to have a member of the hospice team come, verify the death and then call the mortuary.

My friend was unable to accept this. She reprimanded me multiple times for what I had done. To make matters even worse, she discussed it with quite a few people. She went to a professor who taught at our school and asked him for advice about what should be done because I had not left my husband's body sit in my house for two days. She was quite vocal about the whole thing. Not only could she not let it go, but when we discussed that my mother had died, she expressed how good it was that my mother died at home alone and that it took two days until she was found.

In a similar vein, a friend of mine who comes from a traditional Christian background told me how her husband's family was insistent that she play a specific hymn at his funeral services. It was a song that she hated and a song that her husband had hated, too. She stood up to them, and eventually they backed down. But she had to have some very strong communications with them about the fact that he was her husband, the father to her children, and she would be making the final decisions about the services. Eventually, they suggested other hymns and they arrived on one that was acceptable to all.

As you will learn, for MOST people, the concept of death is so uncomfortable that they do not know how to act. Their behaviors are more about their issues with death than they are about helping you. They need to make themselves feel better about death.

On a routine basis, I was questioned about Ed's death. There is a pattern that you will begin to identify. It goes like this:

Q: How old was he?
A. 67

Q: What did he die from
A. Cancer

Q: What kind of cancer?
A. Lung cancer

Q: Was he a smoker?
A. Yes

You can see the thought process roll across someone's face. If they have been a non-smoker, you can see their visible relief. "Phew, dodged a bullet there, this will not happen to me." Which is not true, as I worked with a contractor whose wife, who had never smoked, did, in fact, die from lung cancer.

People need to reconcile with death. They want to know that what happened is not going to happen to them. People adopt a type of death denial, even people who have already encountered death.

Throughout Ed's illness, there was a group that I met with each month. We were part of a mastermind where we would share ideas and support one another in the growth of our respective businesses. We had been meeting for a few years, and it was not unusual to have personal conversations as part of our time together.

Two of the women in the group had been widowed at a young age. As Ed and I progressed together through his cancer, I would mention it. And each time, it was as if it was a surprise. These two specific women, who had been through similar difficult situations, routinely forgot that my husband had stage IV lung cancer. When he died, again, they acted like it was news to them that he had been ill. There was no acknowledgment or recognition of what had transpired. During our conversation, they expressed their condolences, but neither one of them bothered to reach out to me in any personal way, except that when I let them know I was leaving the group, one of them wanted to talk to me about why. I left the group because I could no longer associate with two people who were so unable to offer even a modicum of compassion to me.

Many of the people around you will want you to begin to act "normal" (whatever that means) as soon as possible. In fact, some people will try to respond as if nothing has happened at all. If you even broach the subject, they will pretend that they did not hear you, or redirect the conversation, or tell you that it is time for you to be OK. This is what someone at a party did.

I arrived at the party and knocked on the door. A friend of the hostess opened it. I could see right away that she was uncomfortable. It was almost like she had lost a coin toss or had drawn the short straw. She did the best she could to invite me in and show me where to fix myself a drink. Then she began to stammer out an apology for not contacting me after Ed died. Before I could say the obligatory, "It's OK," or "Don't worry about it," she said, "Well, it's been a few months now, so you should be fine."

And there it was. According to her timetable, I should be over it. So often, what that means is others are over it. Or they want to be over it. At any rate, the time limit that they have invented in their heads has expired. Time to move on. You are no longer allowed to be sad. Don't you dare show emotion or get the least bit teary-eyed, you big baby!

You will find that some people will ghost you. You just will not hear from them. I can think of two people who, to my surprise, have never contacted me. Ed's death notification was the last conversation we ever had. Not a card, not an email, not a text, nothing. As you navigate your own journey through grief, you may find that there are some people who are not worth associating with. Their own inability to be there with you during this time may mean that they do you the favor of taking themselves out of your life. Wish them well, be glad and move on.

In the spirit of honesty, I have been less than helpful to others, too. I am sure that in the past, I said things to people like, "He is in a better place now," or "Everything happens for a reason," or, to my Christian friends, "This must have been part of God's plan." Now I know NONE of that is helpful. And on the receiving end of these comments, you feel yourself stiffen and you brace yourself to smile and hug and get through it.

You have become a member of a club, a not-so-secret society. Once you experience it, you know. And once you experience it, you know that some of your friends and family members want to help you, but they just can't.

People mean well, and they do the best that they can. However, MOST people will not change their behavior just because you are going through a difficult time. If someone is not reliable during the best of times, they will not be reliable during the worst of times.

If someone is unwilling to go out of their way for you during the course of their everyday life, they may not go out of their way for you during a crisis. Some people will help you—on their schedule. This is not unreasonable, but sometimes it is hard to understand why someone's pedicure is the highest priority.

It really does come back to the fact that the people around you might not be able to overcome their own fears and boundaries in order to help you. If you come from a place where you would go out of your way to help a friend, it is hard to understand that a friend would not do the same for you.

For quite some time, I harbored some resentment toward a couple of people who I felt did not step up to the plate to assist me. This was something I really had to sit with. Eventually, I realized that these friends were just being who they were. They had such a fear of death, and such a discomfort with other people's suffering, that they could not fully be there for me. I began to work on sending them compassion during my meditations in order to release my disappointment in their behavior.

When the people around you behave badly, or do not help you through your difficult time, it is most likely because your grief is triggering something within them. They are not reconciled with death and, be-

117

cause they are not reconciled with death, they are not fully available to you.

People do mean well. But you get to decide what is truly helpful to you and what is not. You can turn down help that is not wanted or is not useful. You can decide who you spend time with, and who you avoid.

It is not your job to make other people feel better about your situation. Your work is to take care of yourself and to do what you need to do to recover.

After you experience the death of a loved one, you will never be the same. That is not the same as you will never be OK or you will never be whole. You can emerge from this stronger and with more clarity on how you want to live your life and who you want to be part of your life.

Chapter 19

Some People Will Pleasantly Surprise You

One of Ed's biggest concerns for me was that when he died, I would be alone. He did not believe that I had the right group of friends to help me. He thought that the people who were my closest friends were not going to be there for me. In some cases, he was right. But what he and I did not know was that there would be people who would step up. People who, I would come to understand, cared far more about me than I knew.

You are probably familiar with the expression that people come into your life for a reason, a season or a lifetime. Some of these people are still an essential part of my life today, and some of us have lost touch. Support may not have come from exactly where I expected it, but the good news is that it came.

A year or two before he became sick, Ed formed a very close friendship with a man he met while volunteering. When Ed became sick, this friend stuck by his side. In fact, this friend helped us both. He had seen his mother through terminal illness, and he knew what to expect. He would come by on a Saturday and say, "Margaret, get out of here. I need to spend time with my friend Ed, and we don't want you around." And then, to make sure that I was not offended, he would crack a big smile and give me a big hug. He would also come on Wednesday evenings after work and sit with Ed while I taught an evening class. Sometimes his visits were the only opportunities I had to run errands and take a break. He visited the night that Ed died; in fact, he had only been gone about ten minutes when Ed took his final breath. When I called him, he said, "Well, that is because he wanted to be alone with you during his final moments."

Mom died five days before Ed. There was no way that I could travel to take care of things. I could see that Ed was failing, and there was no way that I would leave him to go to someone who was already dead. I knew he would have died while I was gone. I also knew exactly who to call. My parents had a family friend named Bob, who I admired and trusted. I cannot imagine what I would have done without Bob. He was the one who helped board the window back up (because the sheriff had to break in to the house to find Mom), who took all of the food to be donated (because it was prior to Thanksgiving and Mom was getting ready to host), and who checked on the house and the property for months while it was being sold. The help he gave to me was beyond measure. In fact, Mom's entire community treated me as if I was their own. When I finally was able to come up for the funeral and to begin to close the house, they checked on me; they made sure I had food, and they took me out to dinner.

Mom had always been in love with English gardens. Her garden was amazing. Even at eighty-six years old, she found a way to keep her garden looking beautiful all year round. As she aged, there were some gardening tasks that she could no longer perform. She had a local man who helped her with these tasks. He looked at her as a grandmother. He was heartbroken when she died. Even though I had only met him a time or two, in his way, he took such good care of me. He did not attend her funeral, but when we came back to the house after the funeral, he was waiting for me. He wanted to show me that during her service, he had come to the house and cleaned up the broken glass. He quietly led me to the side of the house, showed me what he had done and then he left.

When I returned about a month and a half later, he met me at the house. He wanted to show me some of the work he had done to keep her plants alive. He would not take any payment. When he learned that I would be staying in the house by myself, he urged me to consider staying elsewhere. He was right; it would have been easier for me if I had listened to him. Staying in that house was one of the hardest things I have ever done. It almost broke me. I kept looking for Mom to come down the hall, or for Dad to be in the kitchen making breakfast, or to go back into the guest room and tell Ed that it was time to wake up. One of the mornings that I was there on my own, I went to the living room to open up the blinds. As I did so, I saw his truck pulling away, and it occurred to me that he had been out there keeping watch over me.

The first person who came to my house after Ed died, aside from hospice and the mortuary staff, was my good friend, who happened to be a Buddhist monk. Some will say, "Well, of course, he is a Buddhist monk, that is his job." But in the past I had seen others who had taken on the holy life falter when it came to dealing with death and dying. He brought me food (croissants as big as my head!), and he checked in on me on a regular basis. If he was going to be in the area, he would make sure that we could meet for coffee or to take a walk.

About three months after your loved one dies, people begin to fall away. MOST people start to fall away before this; it is at the three-month mark when those who were your most active supporters begin to fade away. This monk never forgot about me. Even after three months. Even today.

Ed belonged to a group where he acted as a mentor. I knew of the group but had never met any of them. They were aware of the situation. When Ed died, his close friend notified the group. Most of them had no idea how to contact me. What they did was leave messages on Ed's phone, with the hope that I would receive those messages. I did, and I was so touched by their outpouring of love and support. People I did not even know made some pretty amazing offers of help.

When a classmate asked me to spend a day with her at her Korean Buddhist temple, I readily agreed. Even though most of the day I could not understand one word, I could understand that I was welcome. When my friend told the head nun about what had happened, I could feel her love and compassion in her hug. And at the end of the day, when they divided up the leftover food, they sent me home with a huge care package, which I happily took with me.

A colleague of mine asked if we could meet for coffee once a month or so, just to compare notes about our websites and internet marketing. While we did talk business, I began to understand that this was a respectful way of checking in on me. Without making me feel like a charity case or incompetent, he found a way of getting me to come out of the house and out into the world. In the midst of our discussions on conversion rates and search engine optimization, he would always slip in questions about how I was doing.

Try to be flexible and open to people who are trying to reach out to you. This does not mean that you accept every invitation. For example, a colleague who kept asking me to dinner and a movie less than a month after Ed died, was an easy no thank you. His intentions could have been completely friendly. But it felt off, so I declined.

You will encounter some difficult people. You will also encounter really wonderful people, like the man from the Knights of Columbus who called to tell me that they wanted to provide an honor guard at Mom's funeral, and then stood guard over me while people approached me at Mom's funeral, who made sure that I ate some lunch at the reception that followed. Or the funeral director who thanks you for being so easy to work with, and sends you a card with her personal cell phone, just in case. Or the priest who says your mother's funeral mass and does not give you grief for being a Buddhist. In fact, he slips in a quote from the Dalai Lama about death during his reflections.

This experience of loss is an excellent teacher. A reminder: be careful about the relationships you foster. This is work that you should be doing every day, not just in the midst of a crisis. The decisions you make about the people you keep in your life will hurt you or help you. Pay attention, and you can emerge with strong friends who are worthy of your association.

Your true friends help you even when it is difficult for them to do so. Dealing with death might be challenging, but your friends do the best they can. They look at you with compassion and not down on you with pity. Your friends do not gossip about your misfortune.

Support may not always come from the places you expect, and it may not come in the ways you envision, but the good news is that it will come.

You might not have one person who is consistently there for you. There is a saying, "It takes a village to raise a child." That saying can also be amended to, "It takes a village to lead you through difficult times." In many ways, I had a village and I hope that you do, too.

You will get through this, and you will move on to a new life. You are still alive; make the most of the time you have.

PART VI

NOW WHAT?

Chapter 20

You're Not the
One Who Died

"I used to think that grief was about looking backward, old men saddled with regrets or young ones pondering should-haves. I see now it is about eyes squinting through tears into an unbearable future." – Kate Bowler

Chances are, someone is going to give you a book on the stages of grief, or recommend one to you, or perhaps, if you go to grief counseling, you will become acquainted with the stages of grief. There are some different opinions on the stages and how many there are. There are five stages of grief, or is seven, or is it none? The classic work by Dr. Elizabeth Kubler-Ross covers five stages of grief:

1. Denial
2. Anger
3. Bargaining
4. Depression
5. Acceptance

Some no longer accept this model, and Kubler-Ross herself later regretted that some interpreted her work as five required stages of grief and as a linear set of steps through which every person must pass. The stages she discussed were based on her observations of what people experienced. Not ALL people. Not everyone goes through all of the stages. And even if they do, the stages are not necessarily linear.

Grief is not just a series of events, stages, or timelines. Our society places enormous pressure on us to get over loss, to get through grief. But how long do you grieve for a husband of fifty years, a teenager killed in a car accident, a four-year-old child: a year? Five years? Forever? The loss happens in time, in fact in a moment, but its aftermath lasts a lifetime. *Copyright: Elisabeth Kubler-Ross Family Limited Partnership.*

Some people will talk to you as if going through these five stages is your job. They will ask you questions like, "So what stage of grief are you in now?" Or, they will say things like, "I bet you cannot wait to be finished with your grief stages." Feel free to ignore these people. Feel free to ignore me as I advise you to ignore other people!

Your grief will be your own. We might have some things in common, but our experiences will not be identical. I genuinely believe that having had the opportunity to overcome my fear of death, and to look on death as my carpooling buddy, enabled me to bypass denial and bargaining. Because death was not a surprise to me and I was not inclined to rage against it, I believe that I was in a place of acceptance. I cannot say the same about anger.

When Mom died, one of my early thoughts was, "Really, Mom? You had to be the center of attention, you couldn't just let this be about Ed?" Mother-daughter relationships are complicated. And as much as I was devastated, I was also annoyed.

I did not think that I was angry at Ed. I missed him, I still loved him, I still talked to him. For the first couple of months I kept grocery shopping for him, buying his favorite grape juice and snacks. He was gone, but in many ways I was still in a relationship with him. Then one day, there it was, the anger. It was the weekend that I was by myself at my parents' house in the Pacific Northwest. Of all the things that pushed me to my breaking point, this was the one. To be by myself, taking care of the final business around the house where I had spent so much time with Dad and Mom and Ed was too much. I kept waiting to hear Mom come down the hallway, or to walk into the kitchen and see Dad making us all breakfast, but it was just me. And it was more than I could bear. I remember throwing a book across the room, and bursting into tears. Although I was alone, in between sobs, I yelled at Ed, "You were supposed to be here with me to help with this. I was never supposed to have to do this by myself."

I never minded being in our house by myself. Some people expressed surprise that I was able to stay on my own. Occasionally, people would ask, "So who is staying with you?" In my mind I would snap, "I am a grown woman. I am competent and not an invalid, do you think I need a babysitter?" But out loud I would simply express that I was on my own, and fine with it. And then, lest they get any ideas about sending me a roommate, I would let them know that I preferred living alone. I was happy living with Ed because I loved him. I had no issue living by myself.

Ed was more introverted than I, and there were plenty of times when I would go on outings and he would stay home. After he died, going out to do things with friends was, for the most, part not too difficult. Although there was one time when a friend insisted that I come to a party she was throwing. She insisted that I come by myself. It was the type of event, where Ed would have begrudgingly tagged along with me. When I arrived and found out that the reason she wanted me on my own was that she had plans to set me up with someone, I was not pleased. That was a time where I silently said to Ed, "If you had been here, I would not have had to go through this."

Most of my challenges were not about going places alone; they were about coming home to an empty house. What I missed the most was the way in which he would meet me at the door with a big hug and a kiss. Then he would sit me down and tell me all about whatever he had been reading. Sometimes on the way home from events, I would begin to cry because I knew that Ed would not be there. Other times, if I managed to forget, I would open the door, then immediately feel an overwhelming sadness.

Like it or not, it is time to redefine your life. You do not have to throw away routines that serve you, but it is time to stop buying your husband grape juice and to stop keeping the ingredients for a Brooklyn Egg Cream on hand. Unless you, too, like to drink grape juice and like to make Brooklyn Egg Creams.

Before Ed was diagnosed with cancer, we had been working together to create the next phase in our lives. He was fifteen years my senior, and was beginning to look at retirement. He was working part time, and we were starting to travel more. I was finishing up my course work in my Ph.D. program. To give us more freedom, I was doing less in-person training and more online training. It was this freedom that allowed me to spend an afternoon or two each week with my mother-in-law while she was in assisted living. It was this freedom that had allowed us to be there during Dad's cancer, and to visit Mom more often once she was on her own. It was this freedom that allowed me to be with Ed throughout his cancer. Now here I was, alone, with all of this freedom.

One day, I was sitting in class and our professor started discussing a conference, and how it would be nice if some of us would attend and give presentations. I was sitting next to a friend, and she was going. She turned to me, grabbed my arm and said, "You should come with me." At first, I thought to myself, "I cannot go to Vietnam." But before I said no, another thought quickly replaced "I cannot go to Vietnam," with "Of course I can do this." And so we went. It was a good distraction for me and it helped to deepen our friendship. Since then, we have gone to other conferences together, we visited Taiwan together, and I hope that we will take other trips, too.

The trip to Vietnam encouraged me to go on other adventures. I joined a group of entrepreneurs in the Philippines and on the way home I enjoyed a few days in Seoul. The Korean women that I met were delighted to meet a woman who was traveling on her own. They admired my independence. I was able to laugh when the woman who tidied up my hotel room, put out two pairs of slippers each evening, one in a woman's size and one in a man's size, even though she knew that I was traveling by myself. Just for fun, I took turns wearing the different slippers, moving the man's slippers across the room. Maybe she thought I had a secret boyfriend.

Ed and I had decided that we would travel, and there was no reason for me to stop. Often, I would repeat to myself my mantra of, "I am not the one who died." Every one of my dead family members would have wanted me to keep on going and to live a full life and to be happy. And that is what I am doing. It is what you should do, too.

Just this morning, I was sitting with my sangha. Our teacher was discussing koans, and how the art of questioning can be so beneficial. She asked the group if anyone used koans, and if they wanted to share them with the rest of us. While I am not a Zen practitioner, I realized that, in a way, I did have a koan that I used to inform my life:

"What is my life now?"

"This. This is my life now."

Ready or Not, You Are Redefining Your Life

"There will come a time when you believe everything is finished. That will be the beginning." — Louis L'Amour

When your loved one dies, it is not just the end of their life. It is the end of a part of your life, too. You are still here, you are not the one who died, but now you need to figure out what your life looks like without them.

The good news is that you do not have to do this right away. If you are a person who enjoys routine, you might consider setting up a routine for yourself. Know that this is not going to be your routine forever.

As time passed and I had less of the business of death to attend to, and more strength, I was able to get back to completing more of my work, and I began to regain some of my mental and physical strength. I changed my routine again.

Now my life is a blend of social interactions, professional work, exercise and a bit of travel. I still fine-tune how I spend my time, but what my life is like now is very different from when Ed was alive, and from the first three months after his death, and from even one year after he died.

Your life will change, too. It is a natural evolution.

Do you know what else changes? The way that people treat you and think of you, and the way that you think of yourself. This can be challenging.

Some of the people who were used to you being part of a couple do not know how to treat you. It is unfortunate, but it is true. Some of your couples' friends will fall away. Some women will become insecure because they think that you are after their husbands. Some men will hit on you because they think that as a widow you are desperate for male attention. Of course, in both instances this is wrong and, sadly, these are people who you might miss, but you are better off without them.

The good news is that there will be plenty of people who still see you and who will continue to include you in their plans because they care about you and want to spend time with you. Some people will step down, but others will step up.

It would be untruthful to assume that you have not changed. You have. Your life is different. You see others differently, too.

After I had been on my own for about a year and a half, I began to have a more active social life. Some of this involved dating, but quite a bit of it was getting together with friends for dinners and movies and museum visits and other fun activities. This provoked some interesting behavior in some of the people around me. While most people were supportive, there were a few who were a bit judgmental about it.

I recall being on the receiving end of comments from someone about women of a certain age who were out late at night. The conversation started when an acquaintance of mine wanted me to know that a woman walking in our neighborhood had recently had her purse snatched. The next comment from that acquaintance was, "Well, it was after midnight. Who is out after midnight?"

And at this point, the two of us who were listening to this story both replied with, "College students and teenagers are out after midnight!"

In response, she said, "Well, she was a woman in her fifties, what was she doing out after midnight?"

To which I replied, "Well, I am a woman in my fifties, and I have some friends who are night owls. Often I am out with them until 2 a.m."

Before this, I do not think I had ever seen or heard someone seriously harrumph another person. But that is precisely what this acquaintance did: she harrumphed me. That ended the conversation. This particular person avoided me for several months, and that was a good thing.

Everyone is going to have an opinion about how you should live your life. It is OK to listen to these opinions and to consider them. But in the final analysis, your life is your choice. If you decide that you want to spend the rest of your life in mourning and wear all black like a Sicilian widow, that is an option. If you decide you want to travel or spend your time doing volunteer work that is also an option. No matter what you choose, someone will judge you.

As you rebuild your life, keep an eye out for routines and behaviors that do not serve you well. If you and your loved one used to go to the gym together or walk together, do not abandon exercise just because going to the gym now makes you feel sad. Find a new way to keep an exercise routine in your life. Join a fitness class or walk with a neighbor or change the time of day that you exercise.

Be careful of distractions. When you are going through the grieving process, it is easy to use distractions. I wound up with a Netflix habit and a video game habit that took me several months to break. When I do not know what else to do, I still tend to use work to fill the time. Some people use too much play to avoid dealing with things like cleaning out the closets or going through the paperwork.

At first, you may want to keep things the same. You might want to try to keep the same routines. Be careful with this. Try to select the routines that help you recover and ditch the ones that don't.

Dad used to go to 8:30 a.m. mass every day. Mom was far less regular about it. When Dad died, Mom took over his routine, and she attended 8:30 a.m. mass religiously – pun intended. Somehow, that habit helped her feel close to him, and she enjoyed seeing the people who had seen him at mass each day. From there, she would often have coffee or breakfast with some of this group. This was a new routine. After that, she would run an errand or two. She went to Costco or Walmart or QFC every day.

At first, I thought that going to the store every day was inefficient of her. Why not just keep a list and go once a week, or twice if it was really necessary? This is a perfect example of me making assumptions and judgments about Mom's choices. See, people will do that to you, even your own daughter! Especially your own daughter.

Eventually, I realized that Mom's new schedule was perfect. Mom was extroverted. She loved social gatherings. She loved meeting new people. She loved entertaining. She verbalized most of her thoughts out loud. Her new schedule was perfect—for her! She needed to get out every day and interact with people. When I visited her and went on her routine with her—church, breakfast, errands—I saw how it helped her. She lived in a small town, and at each stop—Costco, Walmart or the QFC—there was someone who knew her and who would usually greet her with a big hug and a smile. When I returned home, the fact that she had that routine was reassuring to me. I knew that she was being loved and cherished by her community.

Pay attention to how you spend your time and ask yourself, "How is this helping me move forward with my life?" And, "Is this something I want to be consistently part of my life?"

Your life is now a do-over. You did not ask for it, but this is what you have. I cannot overemphasize the importance of taking ownership of your life.

Remember, no matter what you choose, someone will judge you. Make sure that you are judged on something that brings you fulfillment. You are not the one who died, so live!

Chapter 21

Pay It Forward

Help Others to Come to Terms with Death

"Why didn't the doctor catch this earlier?" "Why didn't the chemo work?" "Why couldn't they try something else?" "It's not fair that he had to die."

For months after Ed died, one of my friends would circle back to these same questions over and over again. It was exhausting. Part of me wanted to look at her and ask, "Why are you bringing this to me? How do you think this is helping me? And how do you think I can help you with this?"

In her need to make sense of death, she did not realize that her conversation was not useful or helpful to me. It was actually causing me quite a bit of pain. She did not mean to be thoughtless. This was her way of trying to make sense of death, and as her good friend, she wanted to have the conversation with me.

This was not the first time that I had watched her rage against death, and she was not the only person I have seen rage in this way. As you get older, you get closer to death and death gets closer to you. You are going to see people around you die.

I recall a time when my mother, who never wore black (it was not in her color key), decided she needed to shop for a black dress. The funerals were becoming more frequent and she wanted to be appropriately attired. One friend said to me, "I hate this time of life. It seems like the death announcements are coming on a regular basis."

It can be difficult, but why hate this time of life? A friend and Buddhist meditation teacher who used to sit with Ed and I during our hospice phase would say something along the lines of, "The living are dying, and the dying are living." I found this oddly reassuring, a reminder that those who we think are on solid ground can go at any moment and those who we call dying might outlive us. Case in point, Mom who was elderly but in good health died of a heart attack five days before Ed, who was terminally ill. Yes, the living are dying and the dying are living. Technically we are all dying. Death is always with us. We are just more willing to recognize it in the sick and the elderly.

It is better to accept death as another part of life. Understand that you will miss the people you love. You will lose them or they will lose you. The more you stop fighting it, the less power it has over you.

At first, I was hesitant to tell people I was writing about my experiences with death. I thought that most people would say that writing about such a potentially dark topic was not a good idea. I even brought the idea to some mastermind sessions with other entrepreneurs. Most people in the group did not advise me against the topic. No, as typical entrepreneurs, their thoughts were more around how I would monetize this and how I would market it. How could I get people to identify me as an expert, so that they would purchase my book? Most of the group was comfortable with this from an analytical perspective. But once the conversation transitioned from the discussions around blogs and building an audience to the real nitty-gritty of the subject, it was a different story. Some people would begin to become very uncomfortable. You could see the relief on their faces when it was time to move to our next brainstorming session.

Too many people are using avoidance when it comes to the topic of death. Just as people fail to plan for retirement, people fail to plan for death. You might not formally retire, but you are going to die. You do not have to think about it every moment of every day, but why let it be a surprise to you? There will be some deaths that will surprise you by their timing. Mom, dying five days before Ed? Surprising, and yet not surprising. She was eighty-six. She had already lived longer than either of her parents and had outlived both of her siblings. I wanted her to be there for me after Ed died, to help me grapple with being a widow. But there are no guarantees for any of us. Death can seem capricious.

Going back to my friend, the one who continues to rail against death, I have to wonder how much of it is about control. We like to think we have control. We like to think there are rules and promises. Another friend of mine lost her husband when they were still newlyweds. Occasionally she will say, "I did what I was supposed to do. I finished my education and found a husband. Why should this have happened?"

I cannot give her an answer that will make her happy.

To rail against death, and to think that you can control the experiences that come your way, is to cause yourself to suffer even more. The answer is not to avoid life's challenges. Just because you will not look a homeless person in the eye doesn't mean that homeless person does not exist. Ignoring people who are sick does not make them well. Refusing to acknowledge death does not make you or anyone else immortal. The more you wish to avoid suffering, the harder it will be. And the more you crave or want for the people you love to never have to leave you, the more difficult it will be when they do.

You may think, "I will deal with that when the time comes." That is your right. However, this is like choosing to run a marathon with no training. Even though you rarely even jog around the block, you just go out there and attempt to run all twenty-six miles and three hundred and eighty-five yards. You might make it. But it is going to hurt.

"It's not that I'm afraid of dying; it's just that I don't want to be there when it happens!" – Woody Allen

Many of us say things like, "Well, I am OK with my own death, as long as it is quick and painless. I want to die in my sleep." I know because I used to say this, too. There is nothing wrong with wanting an easy death for ourselves or others. But it is not within your control. Death will come when death will come.

You can save yourself a tremendous amount of pain with some preparation. You do not have to walk around obsessed with death, just hold the possibility of death in your thoughts.

One way in which you can make it easy is to accept death as an integral part of life. A way to accept death into your life is to allow yourself to think about it. Don't turn off thoughts about losing others. Don't turn away from people who have experienced loss. Be part of that experience. Go all in.

When it comes to death, there is only one rule. Death. Will. Come.

Be Open to Death

Once you experience death a few times, you become an unofficial death professional. Or, you have the opportunity to do so. It depends on how you go through death. You can be open or closed.

There were two women who I worked with who had both been widowed several years before I met either of them. Despite this, they never offered any personal guidance or wisdom. Each month when I spoke with them, it was always new information to them. "Oh, Ed has cancer? I am sorry to hear that." Yes, you were sorry last month, too. They were closed to the existence of death.

To be closed is to deny the existence of death. The unfortunate result is that when my friend Grim comes to visit, you will be genuinely shocked. I have actually heard people exclaim, "Why did this have to happen?" "Why did he have to die?" In the initial moments of shock, this is understandable. To continue with this thought process well after is only harmful.

My mother had a neighbor who went through an extreme version of death denial. This woman lost her husband to cancer. At that time of his death, he was in his mid-seventies. They had been very close, and his death was devastating to her. Perhaps even more challenging, his death came as a surprise to her. She blamed the doctors for his death. She said they did not do enough to save him. While I do not have her husband's medical records, nor the training to understand them, I do know that sometimes cancer is incurable. This woman spent her final years, and quite a bit of money, suing the doctors and losing. Instead of accepting his death, she fought against it until the time of her own death.

Another version of being closed to death is to refuse to give it any consideration until it is absolutely necessary. Why let an unpleasant topic ruin your day? Why should you face unnecessary sadness by admitting that death will come? Of course, this presupposes that death is bad and unpleasant. It's not easy, but you can prepare. Death is just a process, a stage in our lives. It is our beliefs around it that make it negative. Remember, the Grim Reaper is just doing his job. There is no malice involved on his part. He is an escort.

To refuse to acknowledge death is like knowing you have the toughest final exam of your life coming your way, but you decide to wing it. Or like knowing that you have house guests coming, but since they did not tell you the exact time of their arrival, you decided not to prepare. Then the doorbell rings, and your guests have arrived. And you are not ready.

Mors certa — hora incerta
"Death is certain — the hour is uncertain."

To be open to death is to not be surprised when the doorbell rings and the Grim Reaper is standing on your front porch. Maybe you did not know that today was the day he would arrive, but you have been expecting him. You have discussed his arrival with your friends and family. Depending on who he has come to see, you know what to do. You don't slam the door in his face. By the way, he is the Grim Reaper, I am pretty sure that he can walk through doors. If he rang the bell or knocked, trust me, it was just a formality.

Death is difficult, and many of us come from a culture where we turn our heads away from death. We grit our teeth and get through it. As you get older and have more and more experiences with death, you can choose to accept this as part of your life or you can spend more time in denial or gritting your teeth and getting through it. Is that really how you want to spend the rest of your time? What a waste of energy.

If you can experience death and become accepting instead of turning your back on your experience, then you are open. And when you are open, you can help others around you. This is a pay-it-forward moment. You have been given an experience, and what value is this experience if you do not use it to help others?

You do not have to run around reminding everyone that death is coming, but you can serve as a role model. Once you regain your strength, you can show people that you are not just surviving. You are still alive. You are not sitting on the sidelines. You are out there, living your life in the fullest way possible.

Help show others that widows and widowers and others who have experienced death are not to be pitied. Treated with compassion, absolutely. But do not feel sorry for us. That is condescending. Someone who pities others is expressing that he or she is better off. Think about it, "Oh that poor family has no money for food," or "Have pity on them; they cannot afford rent." Pity involves a comparison.

"Oh, I feel sorry for her; she has no husband," says the woman whose husband is still alive. If death has not come her way yet, she is not better off. She is simply waiting her turn. Do not pity her because she does not understand that death is a 100% guarantee. Be there for her when her time comes. Help her, offer her your compassion and kindness, so that she too can make friends with death.

Help me with a death awareness movement. Help take death out of the darkness. Don't let Grim sit in the corner all by himself. Let him walk next to you, let him join your carpool. And let others learn how to sit next to him in peace.

CONCLUSION

Yo Death, Thanks!
She Says Without a Trace of Irony

"Without sign,
unknown — the life here of mortals —
difficult,
short,
tied up with pain.
For there's no way
by which those who are born
will not die.
Beings are subject
to death
even when they attain
old age.

Like ripe fruits
whose downfall, whose danger
is falling,
so for mortals, once born,
the constant danger
is death."

SN 3.8

In some ways, death has been extremely patient and gentle with me. Some people have lost more of their family and friends much more quickly, some in one single event. Unless you are the first to go, you are going to go through this, too. And as you get older, it will happen more frequently.

The way in which death has been patient and gentle with me is in giving me the lessons that I am sharing with you, and in providing me experiences throughout my life to help me realize that death will come, and that it is going to be OK.

My maternal grandmother died when I was about six. I knew that my mother was really sad and that we would not see grandma again. Death was a vague concept to me. When our little Maltese puppy, Bonnie Muffin Speckleberry, came home blind from the veterinarian and subsequently had to be "put to sleep," I began to get it. A couple of goldfish and my beloved pet mouse, Coffee, really helped me to learn the lesson *"All will go, leaving the body behind."* Of course, I would not have phrased it that way as a child. But that is what I was learning.

The most traumatic lesson I learned was in the first semester of my freshman year of high school. One of my classmates died in an accident on the way to school. If I recall correctly, her brother was driving and was making a left-hand turn. An oncoming car hit them. They might have even been turning into the school parking lot. I am not certain. I am certain that it was the first time that the concept of death became very real to me. I did not know this classmate well. I barely knew her at all. However, as fate would have it, just the day before, she had sat at lunch with a group of us. One day, there she was, the next day, dead before homeroom. It was startling. Death was no longer just for pets and grandparents. Death was for all of us.

In my late twenties, I learned that death could be more drawn out. My favorite aunt, after losing her first husband, met and married a wonderful man. A man who, at fifty, had never been married. And then it became his task to care for his new bride, who slowly became more and more disabled by a progressive neurological disease that would take away her movement and her speech, but only at the very end would it take away her smile.

Yes, death has been gentle and patient with me, teaching me lessons in a skillful way. Starting with the basic concepts, making sure I was paying attention, and then throwing some difficult lessons in for good measure. I saw the emotions that death triggered: the fear, the denial, the disbelief and, sometimes, the anger. I saw how my mother initially tried to avoid her sister's funeral. I saw her become angry with my paternal grandmother when she died a few days before Thanksgiving. I saw a minister refuse to hold the hand of a friend while she was dying. I saw corporate leaders refuse to acknowledge the death of a team member.

Yes, death was teaching me. And now I have learned that there is nothing to fear. Fear is about uncertainty and death is a certainty.

While some people have said to me that I must have terrible karma to have people die so close together, and to be on my own, others have told me that I have been given a tremendous spiritual gift. There is nothing like death to help you understand the Four Noble Truths. All of the lessons that death has taught me have helped me to grow and deepen my practice.

Now I live in this constant state of death awareness. Maybe sometimes I am too aware. Just this morning I took my eighteen-year-old cat to the vet. I was somewhat convinced that this would be the visit, where it would be time to say goodbye. She is very skinny, she is mostly deaf, she might have kidney trouble and now she coughs and hacks for no reason. As I reviewed the symptoms with the veterinarian, she assured me that each of these things could be part of normal aging, and do not mean that her quality of life is completely lacking.

A small battery of tests will tell. But right now, there is no obvious alarming thing. I imagine my cat looking at me and saying, "Relax, I will leave when it is time. Stop trying to kill me off." She has already outlived all of my previous pets, so I am aware and prepared. But that does not prevent me from enjoying my time with her. That is the key message here. Walk with death, but enjoy life.

Without a trace of irony, I can indeed say, "Yo, Death – thanks!"

Thank you for bringing me lessons throughout my life to help me appreciate the gifts I have been given. Thank you for sending me the right people, some to help me through my grief and some to help me understand the behaviors that death triggers in others.

By appearing over and over again, you helped me work through my fear; you have given me strength and the ability to share that strength with others.

The End—For Now.

Based on past experiences and cultural norms, we have each created an image of death. For me, that image has been the Grim Reaper, with his robes and scythe. By making him a character in my life, I learned to accept death and to recognize that life and death go together; they are part of the same experience. By adding him to my carpool, I humanized him and made him less frightening. He's just another interesting character in my life.

The concept of carpooling with death, and of referencing the character of Death as created by Terry Pratchett, was a helpful way for me to process my feelings about what felt like a steady stream of loss. By animating death, I was able to acknowledge it as a constant companion.

The *Alagaddupama Sutta* is a popular teaching that reminds us not to cling to views that help us along the path:

"*Suppose a man were traveling along a path. He would see a great expanse of water, with the near shore dubious and risky, the further shore secure and free from risk, but with neither a ferryboat nor a bridge going from this shore to the other. The thought would occur to him, 'Here is this great expanse of water, with the near shore dubious and risky, the further shore secure and free from risk, but with neither a ferryboat nor a bridge going from this shore to the other. What if I were to gather grass, twigs, branches, and leaves and, having bound them together to make a raft, were to cross over to safety on the other shore in dependence on the raft, making an effort with my hands and feet?' Then the man, having gathered grass, twigs, branches, and leaves, having bound them together to make a raft, would cross over to safety on the other shore in dependence on the raft, making an effort with his hands and feet. Having crossed over to the further shore, he might think, 'How useful this raft has been to me! For it was in dependence on this raft that, making an effort with my hands and feet, I have crossed over to safety on the further shore. Why don't I, having hoisted it on my head or carrying it on my back, go wherever I like?' What do you think, monks: Would the man, in doing that, be doing what should be done with the raft?'*

"'No, lord.'

"And what should the man do in order to be doing what should be done with the raft? There is the case where the man, having crossed over, would think, 'How useful this raft has been to me! For it was in dependence on this raft that, making an effort with my hands and feet, I have crossed over to safety on the further shore. Why don't I, having dragged it on dry land or sinking it in the water, go wherever I like?' In doing this, he would be doing what should be done with the raft." - MN 22

The scary persona created around death, the Grim Reaper, has no place in Buddhism. Making a personality out of Grim is making too much of death.

My use of the Grim Reaper as a character and as my carpool companion is like the raft. I built this analogy and walked around thinking about it, and visualizing my friend the Grim Reaper because it helped me to become comfortable with death. He became someone I knew, who had a job to do. Like anyone else, he is just taking care of business. There is nothing more to it.

The more comfortable I become with my friend Grim, and the more accustomed I am to integrating death into my life, the less often I will need him to be my carpool partner. Soon I will be able to drop him off. Not because he will be gone for good, but because I won't need to see him in the passenger seat to understand that death is always along for the ride. He will have served his purpose.

About the Author

Margaret Meloni is a Buddhist practitioner and a new voice on the subject of death awareness. *Carpooling with Death* is her debut work. She might carpool with the Grim Reaper, but she wishes that he would stay out of her kayak and off her paddleboard. Especially when he is not willing to do any of the work! Her two cats teach her humility and subservience on a regular basis. To find out what is next for Margaret, be sure to visit www.margaretmeloni.com/carpoolingwithdeath/.

Made in United States
North Haven, CT
23 December 2021

13559908R00090